WORDS AND DEEDS

Words and Deeds

Problems in the Theory of Speech Acts

DAVID HOLDCROFT

> Words and deeds are quite indifferent
> modes of the divine energy.
> Words are also actions, and actions are
> a kind of words.
>
> (Emerson, *Essays*, xiii)

1478
1978

CLARENDON PRESS · OXFORD

Oxford University Press, Walton Street, Oxford OX2 6DP

OXFORD LONDON GLASGOW NEW YORK
TORONTO MELBOURNE WELLINGTON CAPE TOWN
IBADAN NAIROBI DAR ES SALAAM LUSAKA ADDIS ABABA
KUALA LUMPUR SINGAPORE JAKARTA HONG KONG TOKYO
DELHI BOMBAY CALCUTTA MADRAS KARACHI

© *David Holdcroft 1978*

British Library Cataloguing in Publication Data

Holdcroft, David
  Words and deeds.
  1. Semantics (Philosophy)
  I. Title
  149'.94   P325   77–30411

ISBN–0–19–824581–5

Printed in Great Britain by
Billing & Sons Ltd, Guildford, London and Worcester

For Aku

ACKNOWLEDGEMENTS

I AM indebted to many people for their help and advice. My colleagues at Warwick made many useful suggestions in seminars on drafts of various chapters. Many other friends commented on preliminary drafts, or helped me with points that worried me. I would like to thank especially Martin Bell, Kit Fine, Peter Gardner, Peter Mott, Anthony Price, and Stephen Read. Finally, my thanks to Jean Fife, the accuracy of whose typing is uncanny, and to Alun Jones for his help with the proofs.

DAVID HOLDCROFT

University of Warwick,
December 1976

CONTENTS

INTRODUCTION

THE CENTRAL theme of this work is the nature of illocutionary acts. The theme is, as I see it, a limited one, since I do not think that the concept of an illocutionary act can be used to elucidate the fundamental notions in the philosophy of language of meaning and truth, a position I argue for in part in Chapters 2 and 3. Hence, many of the most important issues in the philosophy of language lie outside the scope of this work. Nevertheless, the fact that a sentence with a given meaning has, in virtue of the fact that it has that meaning, a potentiality for a certain range of uses is one of great importance. It is because this is so that a theory of use is rooted in, though it does not reduce to, a theory of meaning. If it were not so rooted, then a sentence's meaning would place no constraint on its range of uses, and the third member of the venerable trio of syntax, semantics, and pragmatics would be quite independent of the other two. How, if this were so, one would, on a given occasion, know what speech act a speaker was performing by the literal utterance of a sentence would be something of a mystery, and, in the absence of a correlation between ranges of uses and sentence-types, so would language learning. My primary aims are, therefore, firstly, to give an account of the relation between a given sentence-type and a certain range of speech acts, and, secondly, to say what is involved in performing a speech act within this range.

One thing I assume is that one task for a semantic theory of L is to recursively ascribe truth conditions to each of the indicative sentences of L. It is not necessary for my purposes to make the stronger assumption that a theory which does this *is* a theory of meaning for L. The stronger assumption is indeed so controversial that it would hardly be reasonable to make it without argument. By contrast, the weaker assumption I do make, which says nothing about what a theory of meaning is, seems an acceptable one since it commands very widespread assent. Secondly, I assume that, as Hare and others have argued, a sentence's mood is an aspect of its meaning. Indeed, it seems clear that a sentence's mood is a partial determinant of the sorts of illocutionary acts it can be used literally to perform. But what is a mood?

I am, and have been for some time, attracted by the identification of the indicative mood with the possession of truth conditions.[1] The identification is attractive because it seems clear that the fact that a sentence has truth conditions places a restriction on the range of speech acts it can be used literally to perform, and given the first assumption made above, one task of a semantic theory of L is to recursively ascribe truth conditions to the indicative sentences of L. Moreover, it seems that the restrictions placed on the range of speech acts which a sentence can be used literally to perform by the fact that it has truth conditions is the same as that placed by the fact that it is in the indicative mood. So, it would appear, a theory which has ascribed truth conditions to the indicative sentences of L does not have to go on to perform an additional task, that of giving an account of the indicative mood by, for example, proposing the existence of a morpheme with some such interpretation as 'may be asserted'. There are not two separate tasks here, but only one. If this is so, then the truth conditions of a sentence are determinants both of its logical form and of its mood, and hence partial determinants of literal utterances of it.

The questions whether similar proposals can be defended in the case of other sentences-types is a difficult one, which is discussed in Chapters 5–7. I there argue against analyses of the kind proposed by Hare[2] and others according to which different sentence-types have a major element in common, a sentence-radical or phrastic, and differ only in the kind of sentence operator or neustic they contain. Though these analyses appear to offer impressive gains in the simplification of semantic theory it turns out that the appearance is illusory. Further, it seems clear that various ways of 'reducing' imperatives to indicatives fail, e.g., the suggestion that 'Shut the door' is tantamount to 'The speaker wishes you to shut the door.' Detailed criticism apart, theories of this sort get things the wrong way round. The

---

[1] I argued this in a paper given to the 1973 York Conference on Logic and Semantics.
[2] See, for instance. Hare (1952).

proper emphasis should be on what the intended audience has to do to conform, not on what the speaker wants it to do. Hence the fact that the characteristic criticism of an act performed by literal utterance of an imperative is not of the commander, but of the intended audience for failing to do what it was enjoined to do.

Nevertheless, there are grounds for unease with the position which I adopt that imperatives have conformity conditions to which they are related as indicatives are to truth conditions. For this view not only seems to leave the meanings of the logical constants in imperatives unconnected with their meanings in indicatives, but it threatens to render unintelligible a host of important, if humdrum, connections, between indicatives and imperatives. For instance, if a command given by literal use of 'Shut the door!' has been conformed with, then it is true that the door is shut; and if the command can be conformed with, but has not yet been, then the door is open. But if conformity conditions are not truth conditions, it might well be argued that these claims are far from trite and obvious.

However, since in claiming that imperatives have conformity conditions I only mean to claim that to understand an imperative one must know what state of affairs the intended audience must produce in order to conform with a speech act performed by uttering the imperative literally, these points can be met. For if having specified what conformity is in the simplest (atomic) case in such a way that if 'Shut the door!' has been conformed with, then the door has been shut by a certain person, we can go on to specify, for example, that 'Either shut the door or shut the window!' is conformed with if either 'Shut the door!' or 'Shut the window!' is (or both). The meanings of the logical constants in imperatives will, therefore, be parasitic on their meanings in indicatives, since the former will have been explained wholly in terms of the latter. On this account, indicatives will have a certain logical primacy, since they will be required to state the conditions under which an imperative is conformed with; but imperatives will not be 'reducible' to indicatives unless, as seems unlikely, conformity is reducible to truth.

Granted that imperatives have conformity conditions, then interrogatives can be treated as a special kind of imperative, and, where appropriate, different sorts of conditions can be associated with other sentence-types. It is then possible to associate a certain range of illocutionary acts with the literal utterance of sentences of each of these types in such a way that it follows that if a speaker is performing any illocutionary act at all, then he is performing one that falls within this range. So the connection between a given sentence-type and illocutionary act is this: the sentence-type depends on what type of condition is involved in the semantic interpretation of the sentence, and this in turn partially determines the nature of the illocutionary acts performed by literal utterances of it.

However, the determination is only partial; what specific illocutionary force an utterance has depends on the intentions of the speaker, and what illocutionary *act* is performed, if any, depends on these in part, but also on features of the context of utterance. The speaker's intentions alone cannot suffice to ensure, for instance, that his utterance is a report. If it is, then he must be, or have been, a privileged observer.

The account of illocutionary acts which I propose in Chapter 8 makes a sharp distinction between those features of an utterance in virtue of which it is correlated by means of truth or conformity conditions with a certain possible state of affairs, and those features of its context which are the intended or actual determinants of the illocutionary act performed. Secondly, it allows for the possibility that the presence of such determinants of an illocutionary act may be indicated by an appropriate device (e.g. a performative prefix), but it does not stipulate that they must be so indicated. Thirdly, it places an implicit restriction on the intended force of an utterance by, in effect, requiring the speaker to believe that his audience can determine what the intended force is by observing features of the context of utterance. And, fourthly, since, in most cases anyway, what illocutionary act is performed depends crucially on the presence or absence of certain features in the context of utterance, it follows that the question whether, for example, someone's utterance was a report can no more be settled simply by considering his intentions and the meanings of his words than the question whether what he said is true. Thus, given the first point, the same sentence can often be used to perform different illocutionary acts, which permits a flexible, and even innovatory, use to be made of it. Given the second point, intended illocutionary force may be conventionally indicated, but it does not have to be—which accords with the fact that illocutionary force often does not seem to be conventionally indicated—though according to the third point the speaker must believe that it is determinable from features of the context of utterance. Finally, in most cases, anyway, what act the speaker performs depends on the presence or absence of these features.

The most difficult problem remains, namely, 'What are these features?'. They cannot, I believe, be delineated in precise terms, but if attention is restricted to acts performed by the literal utterance of an indicative the general nature of what is relevant becomes clear.

Typically, the problem of an audience is to decide what beliefs to adopt or change, and what courses of action to take, etc., on the basis of what is said to it. Its task would be made very much easier if it could assume that every indicative sentence uttered literally and seriously in its presence expressed something to which the speaker was unreservedly committed. Even if it could assume this, the problem of sincerity would remain; but obviously unreserved commitment cannot be assumed. An utterance may express what is from the speaker's point of view only an hypothesis, or a suggestion, etc. So the first question which has to be settled is whether the speaker is committed unreservedly, or only qualifiedly, to the truth of what he says; and this corresponds to one important dimension of illocutionary force.

Unfortunately, by no means everything a speaker is fully committed to is worthy of belief, even if the speaker's sincerity is not in doubt. The question whether it is is, therefore, a further question to which an audience has to address itself. Here many sub-divisions exist. Was the speaker in a position to observe at first hand, or, at least, to obtain information from a reliable source? If he was, then what he says is, assuming sincerity, worthy of serious consideration. Then there are questions about the way in which the speaker arrived at his opinion. Was calculation or diagnosis involved? Did he make an inference, and if so from what did he infer his conclusion? Knowing the answer to these questions obviously puts one in a much better position to decide whether to adopt the speaker's belief. The calculation can be checked, and the validity of the inference examined, etc. so that some estimate can be made of the probability of error and of the plausibility of the conclusion. Also, the question whether the speaker is an authority is important; if he is, then what is said at least merits serious consideration. These kinds of consideration correspond to a second major dimension of illocutionary force; and we can readily add two further dimensions. One involves the nature of the claim made, i.e. what is relevant to its confirmation and disconfirmation. Is it, for instance, more specific than the claim that X is Y, in that what is being claimed is that what is characteristic of X is that it is Y? If it is, then a number of criticisms are relevant which would not be relevant to the claim *simpliciter* that X is Y. The final dimension discussed, though no doubt there are others, is a rather humdrum one which involves keeping track of the relation of what the speaker says to other speech acts of his own and of his audience. It makes a good deal of difference, for instance, if something is merely an interpolated comment rather than a reply.

It is not difficult to see how, in principle, a feature matrix indicating the absence or presence of features in each of these dimensions might be used to characterize a large number of illocutionary acts performable by literal utterance of an indicative. Admittedly, given the relative vagueness of some of the dimensions it would not be a very tidy matrix, and its comprehensiveness would always be questionable, but the principles behind its construction are clear.

However, the most important remaining argument is not one about the comprehensiveness of my proposed scheme, but one which, if sustainable, threatens to undermine it completely. I would like, therefore, to try to state the argument as clearly as I can, and say why I think it fails.

Confining attention, for the sake of simplicity, to indicatives, the theory proposed takes the fact that an indicative has truth conditions to explain why it can be used literally to perform a certain range of illocutionary acts, though it does not, of course, explain why the sentence is used to perform some one act within that range on a given occasion rather than some other. This can be summarized by saying that the possession of truth conditions by a sentence is a weak determinant of illocutionary force. But what are truth conditions? May it not be that one can only explain the notion of a truth condition in terms of the very illocutionary acts which, according to me, a sentence which has truth conditions may be used literally to perform? But if that were so, our initial explanation would appear to be empty. For the possession of truth conditions by a sentence would, according to me, explain why it can be used literally to perform a certain range R of illocutionary acts; but what it is to have truth conditions would have to be explained by reference to the very illocutionary acts which belong to the range R.

Whilst he probably would not wish to put the difficulty in terms as bald as these, it seems that Strawson was the first to raise the issue discussed here in a sharp form,[3] namely, whether the notion of a truth condition is independent of that of the notions of such illocutionary acts as assertion, prediction, and supposition, which I will hereafter call 'statemental acts'. Since I claim that the possession by a sentence of truth conditions is a weak determinant of illocutionary force I am, of course, committed to maintaining that the notion of a truth condition is *not* completely independent of that of the statemental acts. On the other hand, my account would lapse into vacuity if the notions of the statemental acts had to be used to explain that of a truth condition; so I must deny that this is so. Since these issues are ones which arise in Strawson's discussion, I would like to expand on them further by reference to it.

Strawson is concerned with a rough contrast between theorists of communication-intention and theorists of formal semantics. The former claim that 'it is impossible to give an adequate account of the concept of meaning without reference to the possession by speakers of audience directed intentions of a certain complex kind',[4] viz., those involved in an analysis of such locutions as 'By uttering x S meant that p'. The theorists of formal semantics, by contrast, maintain that 'the system of semantic and syntactical rules, in the mastery of which knowledge of a language consists—the rules which determine the meanings of sentences—is not a system of rules *for* communicating at all.'[5] Strawson's main concern is to argue that one influential theory, which he regards as being of this second sort,

[3] See Strawson (1970).
[4] Strawson (1970), p. 4.
[5] Strawson (1970), p. 5.

is not, though it may seem to be, independent of a theory of communication. The theory, argued for by Davidson, claims that a theory of truth in *L* which ascribes truth conditions to each of the sentences of *L is* a theory of meaning for *L*. Now Strawson does not seem to wish to deny that *one* thing a theory of meaning for *L* should be able to do is to recursively ascribe truth conditions to the sentences of *L*, a point which is of some importance. But he does ask 'whether the notion of truth conditions can itself be explained without reference to the function of communication',[6] and argues that it cannot.

His argument proceeds on the assumption that 'most of the weight of a general theory of meaning and of particular semantic theories, falls on the notion of truth conditions . . .';[7] but what can we say about truth *in general*? Strawson suggests that we can at least maintain this:[8]

(1) One who makes a $\left\{ \begin{array}{l} \text{assertion} \\ \text{statement} \\ \text{supposition} \end{array} \right\}$ makes a true

$\left\{ \begin{array}{l} \text{assertion} \\ \text{statement} \\ \text{supposition} \end{array} \right\}$ if and only if things are as, in making that

$\left\{ \begin{array}{l} \text{assertion} \\ \text{statement} \\ \text{supposition} \end{array} \right\}$ he $\left\{ \begin{array}{l} \text{asserts} \\ \text{states} \\ \text{supposes} \end{array} \right\}$ them to be.

And if, as we have assumed, meaning is determined by truth conditions, then we can also claim:

(2) The meaning of a sentence is determined by the rules

which determine *what* $\left\{ \begin{array}{l} \text{assertion} \\ \text{statement} \\ \text{supposition} \end{array} \right\}$ is made by one

who, in uttering the sentence in given conditions,

expresses a $\left\{ \begin{array}{l} \text{assertion} \\ \text{statement} \\ \text{supposition} \end{array} \right\}$

But the truth of (2) gives, Strawson argues, the communication-theorist his chance. He sees that the consideration of the

[6] Strawson (1970), p. 13.

[7] Strawson (1970), p. 14.

[8] The following is, if true, true of all statemental acts, of which the bracketed items are but a sample.

notion of truth leads to that of the content of the statemental acts, but sees no hope of elucidating this without elucidating the notions of the acts themselves. But this brings in audience-directed intentions, so that the thesis that meaning is to be elucidated in terms of truth conditions, 'far from being an alternative to a communication theory of meaning, leads us straight in to such a theory of meaning'.[9]

But what precisely is Strawson claiming? That the notion of truth 'leads to' the notions of the statemental acts might mean no more than:

(3) If a sentence x has truth conditions, then it can be used literally to perform any one of the statemental acts.

Now that (3) is true is something I accept, since it describes the crucial link between truth conditions on the one hand, and the statemental acts on the other. It is because there is this connection that it is reasonable to take the statemental acts which a person performs as evidence, assuming both sincerity and literalness of use, of his beliefs about the truth conditions of the sentence he used. Hence, for instance, the point of the strategy adopted by Quine's jungle linguist who is interested precisely in the sorts of circumstances in which a native is prepared to assent to, or dissent from, a sentence. And if, as I believe, no stronger connection can be described between truth conditions and the statemental acts, it is easy to see why Quine's linguist should be faced with problems of 'intrusive' belief, of under-determination, and so on. So though the connection described by (3) may not seem to be a very impressive one, it is an extremely important one.

However to grant (3) is no more to grant that

(4) The concept of truth can be explained in terms of the concept of particular statemental acts (e.g. assertion),

than it is to grant that

(5) The concept of each statemental act can be explained in terms of truth alone.

No one would, I think, wish to maintain (5), so the crucial question is whether (4) is true. If it is, then the *explanatory* value of (3) would be slight indeed. If, on the other hand, (3) is true, and both (4) and (5) are false, then the way in which 'we are led, by way of the notion of truth, back to the notion of the

[9] Strawson (1970), p. 16.

content of such acts as stating, expressly supposing, and so on'[10] would hardly show that it was improper in a theoretical exposition to begin by explaining meaning in terms of truth conditions. For the truth of (3) would assure us that once we had done so we could go on smoothly to give an account of the acts which a sentence with truth conditions can be used literally to perform. To say this is not to deny, of course, that to construct a theory of meaning for a particular language one will have to take into account the statemental acts which speakers of that language perform. I see no reason to doubt that these will provide indispensable evidence guiding the construction of the theory. But the fact that this is so does not mean that truth can be explained by reference to those acts, any more than the fact that the behaviour of players on a football field provides evidence of their beliefs about the rules of the game means that those rules can be defined in terms of notions descriptive of that behaviour. Of course, if (4) were true things would be quite different; so the question of the truth of (4) is an important one.

Following Strawson in concentrating attention on assertion as a central statemental act, it seems very unclear whether the truth of:

(6) One who makes an assertion makes a true assertion if and only if things are as in making that assertion he asserts them to be,

establishes the truth of (4), not, of course, that Strawson suggests that it does. A small point to begin with: an instance of (6) is presumably:

(7) One who asserts that it is raining makes a true assertion if and only if things are as in making that assertion he asserts them to be.

But since if things are as in making that assertion he asserts them to be, then it is raining, and *vice versa*, then (7) is equivalent to:

(7') One who asserts that it is raining makes a true assertion if and only if it is raining.

And since one who asserts that it is raining makes a true assertion if and only if the assertion that it is raining is true, (7') is equivalent to:

(7") The assertion that it is raining is true if and only if it is raining.

[10] Strawson (1970), p. 15.

In (7″) 'assertion' has its object sense, so that the connection with the notion of an assertive act has become tenuous. That this should be so is, incidentally, hardly surprising if it is conceded that *what* someone asserts when he utters a sentence of *L* literally is determined by the rules of truth for *L*. Thus, the claim that a theory of truth for *L* has as consequences all instances of the schema:

(8) The assertion that *p* is true if and only if *p*

is a claim which is as general as (6), but which much less clearly involves the notion of an assertive act.

Secondly, (6) could hardly be treated as a definition of truth since it gives no account of what it is for suppositions, predictions, etc. to be true. The obvious retort is that truth is to be defined by reference to the battery of statemental acts mentioned in (1), but this fails unless the class of statemental acts is a well-defined totality. The natural way of defining membership in the class would be to say that they are acts which have an object which is true or false; but this is obviously blocked if the strategy is to define truth in terms of the statemental acts.

Thirdly, (6) would underpin (4), and perhaps constitute a partial definition of truth, only if the notion of an assertive act could itself be explicated without reference to that of truth, or, at least, if it is possible to have a concept of assertion without having one of truth. *Prima facie* the two concepts are much too closely linked for this to be possible, since to assert that *p* is to assert that *p* is true. Hence, the attractiveness of the theory that assertion is a speech act governed by a social convention of truth telling, as Dummett has argued:

there has to be some feature of the sentences which signify their being uttered with assertoric force; and an account of the significance of this feature—and thus of the activity of making assertions—is to be given by describing the convention under which sentences possessing this feature are used. We described this convention in a quite summary way, by merely saying that the convention was to utter such sentences with the intention of uttering only true ones.[11]

An approach such as this admits of many variations, and is not without its difficulties. But it is clearly not possible on this approach, whatever the variation, to take assertion as given, and then go on to define truth in terms of it, i.e. to produce a classical

[11] Dummett (1973), p. 354.

analysis in which the *definiendum* is the notion of truth and the *definiens* involves that of assertion. However, though truth may not be definable in terms of assertion, it does not follow that there is no connection whatsoever between them, which might well be regarded as an unacceptable conclusion. As urged earlier there is the connection described by (3), and the existence of this connection makes it reasonable to take the fact that a man is prepared to assert a sentence in some circumstances but not in others as evidence of his beliefs about its truth conditions. So the denial that truth can be explained in terms of assertion does not render unintelligible the practice of taking a person's willingness to utter a sentence x in certain sorts of circumstances as evidence of his beliefs about the truth conditions of x.

A different approach to the analysis of assertion, which Dummett rejects, maintains that an assertion is essentially the expression of a belief; to assert p is, speaking roughly, to give an audience a certain sort of reason for thinking that one believes that p. Hence, if belief could be explained without reference to truth, and assertion explained in this sort of way, then it might very well be possible to explain truth non-circularly in terms of assertion.

Now if there are purely behavioural criteria of belief, then it might, at first sight, seem possible to explain belief without reference to truth. Might we not, on the basis of certain behaviour, attribute a belief that he is going for a walk to a dog, and yet hesitate to attribute to him the belief that it is true that he is? Perhaps we might; but the crucial issue is not whether a belief that p is always a belief that p is true, but whether we can suppose a creature to have a concept of belief (as well as particular beliefs), who does not have a concept of truth. It is difficult to believe that we can, for considerations of truth and falsity seem to be essentially involved in the ascription of beliefs to another. It is because the dog behaves in a 'walk-expecting' manner when he is indeed going for a walk, or when there is good reason to suppose that a walk is in the offing, and is known to be capable of modifying that behaviour if certain sorts of clear signs turn up that there will not be a walk after all, that it seems reasonable to attribute the belief to him. In other words, it is because a certain pattern of behaviour is correlated with situations in which there will be a walk, or in which there is good reason to suppose that there will be, and absent in situations in which there is no such reason, that it seems reasonable to take the presence of the behaviour as evidence that the dog believes that he is to go for a walk. Indeed, it is difficult to see why one should attribute any one belief rather than any other to someone on the basis of behaviour of his unless one made use of the regulative notion of truth. Scepticism that a certain kind of behaviour constitutes evidence of a belief that a walk is in the offing is amply justified if the pattern of behaviour is in no way modified in the presence of clear evidence that there will be no walk. So one could not attribute a concept of belief to a creature whom one did not think had one of truth. For to apply his concept he would have to ascribe beliefs to others and to do this he would have to have a concept of truth. It might be questioned whether to have a concept of belief one has to be able to apply it to others, but in the present context there is no need to enter into such a controversy. For the proposed analysis of assertion as the expression of a belief attributes a complex audience-directed intention to the speaker, the intention that his audience should have a certain sort of belief as a result (in part) of recognizing his intention. But to have this intention the speaker must think that it can be realized. In which case he must suppose it possible for his audience to have beliefs, and to do this he must have a concept of truth.

This discussion is inevitably somewhat inconclusive, since there are very probably other approaches to the analysis of assertion which we have overlooked. However, we have seen no grounds for accepting (4), and many for rejecting it. Indeed, the case for its rejection seems to be overwhelmingly strong. Its rejection removes my general position from any taint of circularity, whilst the assertion of (3) allows for the sort of connection between the possession of truth conditions and the statemental acts which language learning strategies presuppose. Finally, in urging the truth of (3) I do not wish to seem to suggest that a linguistic community could first formulate a concept of truth, and then go on to devise a practice of asserting things to be true. The claim that (3) is true, together with the further claim, which I would urge, that if it has a practice of assertion then it has a concept of truth, is not meant to have any temporal implications.

CHAPTER 1

MANY DIFFERENT languages having the feature of a natural language, such as English, can be conceived of. That is, languages which can be learnt by someone who does not already possess a language, contain indefinitely many sentences, and which can be used to talk about a very wide range of subject matters. Some of these languages will be very unlike English; but one would find it as difficult to conceive of one which could not be used to do such things as make assertions, give orders, and ask questions, as one would to conceive of one which had no grammar. Presumably, this is so because a potentiality for a certain sort of use is as much an essential feature of a language as is the possession of a grammar.

If, following J. L. Austin, asserting, ordering, questioning, etc. are called 'illocutionary acts',[1] then this point could be made by saying that a language must be such that it can be used to perform illocutionary acts. Not that this would be an uncontroversial way of making the point, for the viability of Austin's notion has been hotly disputed. If the point made in this way is to be defended, it is necessary, therefore, to rebut various attacks on the Austinian notion, and, more positively, to develop a detailed theory of the nature of illocutionary acts, for it is clear that Austin did not succeed in doing so. Of course, if there are such acts, then many questions about them arise. How are the illocutionary acts a speaker performs related to the sentences he utters? What constraints does a sentence of a language place on the range of acts that a speaker can perform by uttering it? What, if anything, do meaning and syntax separately contribute towards these constraints? And what finally does a speaker have to do to perform different sorts of illocutionary acts?

If these and related questions could be answered, then the relation between language and speech would be much clearer than it is. No doubt on any view a theory of speech will be more

[1] Austin (1962), pp. 98 ff.

extensive than a theory of illocutionary acts; but a theory of illocutionary acts will be an essential ingredient in such a theory, since one cannot say something without performing some illocutionary act or other. Moreover, it is highly desirable to have as clear a picture of the relation between language and speech as possible. For whilst it is undoubtedly correct to conceive of a language in an abstract way as a set of syntactical, semantical, and phonological rules, conceived of like this it does not seem to have much connection with what speakers do with it. Yet surely there must be such a connection; a point at which a language makes contact with the 'world', giving rise to claims and queries about what actually is the case, about which, of course, the language itself 'says' nothing.

Hopefully then, a theory of illocutionary acts will throw some light on this point of connection. But before trying to show that it does, it seems sensible to examine briefly Austin's conception of an illocutionary act, inadequate though it is. For if it is misconceived in principle in certain ways that have been alleged,[2] then the project of using a theory of illocutionary acts to illuminate the connection between a language, conceived of in abstract terms, and some of the things its speakers do with it must be misconceived from the start.

1. AUSTIN'S DISTINCTIONS

Austin introduces the notion of an illocutionary act as part of a comprehensive theory of speech acts in which he distinguishes three kinds of act, locutionary, illocutionary, and perlocutionary. But the nature of the distinction between both the first and the second kind of act, and the second and third kind, is far from clear.

(i) Consider the first distinction; a locutionary act, Austin maintains, includes 'the utterance of certain words in a certain construction, and the utterance of them with a certain "meaning" in the favourite philosophical sense of that word, i.e. with a certain sense and reference'.[3] He plainly thought it possible for someone to know what locutionary act had been performed on a given occasion without knowing what illocutionary act had

---

[2] See L. J. Cohen (1964), and Searle (1968).
[3] Austin (1962), p. 94.

been performed, that is, without knowing with what force the words uttered were used:

it might be perfectly possible with regard to an utterance, say 'It is going to charge', to make entirely plain 'what we are saying' in issuing the utterance, in all the senses so far distinguished, and yet not at all to have cleared up whether or not in issuing the utterance I was performing the act of *warning* or not.[4]

This is possible apparently because 'to determine what illocutionary act is . . . performed we must determine in what way we are using the locution'.[5] Another feature of the illocutionary act to which Austin plainly attached importance is its conventionality.[6] So what apparently distinguishes the illocutionary from the locutionary act is the fact that the former, but not the latter, involves some special conventionally determined way of using words.

But if by calling an illocutionary act 'conventional' Austin intended to claim that one has to comply with the sort of procedure that has to be complied with to get married, or to make a legal will, then many frequently cited examples of illocutionary acts are not conventional, e.g. warnings, protests, entreaties.[7] And though it may be true that one can sometimes know with what sense and reference certain words were uttered, without knowing what force their utterance had, it is far from clear that this epistemological point grounds a distinction between different sorts of acts. After all, may I not know that a man has made a cube without knowing that he has made a six-sided figure? But it hardly follows that to make a cube is to do something different from making a six-sided figure. Moreover, Austin's initial characterization of locutionary acts can be no clearer than the notions of sense and reference he uses, and these are certainly problematical since he never says what the extension of either is. Thus, it is arguably consistent with his remarks to count the reference of 'I' and the sense of both 'I' and 'maintain' as part of the sense and reference of 'I maintain that he is there.'

---

[4] Austin (1962), p. 98.
[5] Austin (1962), ibid.
[6] Austin (1962), p. 103.
[7] That is, a procedure which can be described by some set of (A) and (B) rules as outlined in Lecture II of Austin (1962). The general point was first made in Strawson (1964).

But if this is done, it might seem that there is no hope of distinguishing the locution (a sentence with a determinate sense and reference) from the illocution (the force of an utterance of a sentence with a definite sense and reference).[8]

(ii) One can, Austin maintains, perform a perlocutionary act, as one can an illocutionary act, by using a locution; but the type of use is different.

Saying something will often, or even normally, produce certain consequential effects upon the feelings, thoughts, or actions of the audience, or of the speaker, or of other persons: and it may be done with the design, intention, or purpose of producing them; and we may then say, thinking of this, that the speaker has performed an act in the nomenclature of which reference is made either only obliquely, or even not at all, to the performance of the locutionary or illocutionary act.[9]

Thus, a perlocutionary act is performed when someone's saying something (an illocutionary act) has a certain consequence, either intended or unintended. It is not entirely clear whether Austin thought that it is necessary to perform an illocutionary act to perform a perlocutionary one. Certainly, he allowed that perlocutionary effects can be produced without performing an illocutionary act; and it is clearly possible to employ a concept of a perlocutionary act which classes as such various acts which have perlocutionary consequences, even though they are not illocutionary acts,[10] which is what I shall do in what follows.

In the course of trying to distinguish the two sorts of act Austin repeatedly asserts that whilst an illocutionary act is essentially conventional[11] a perlocutionary act is not. Further, whilst the vast majority of perlocutionary effects can be produced by non-verbal means, most illocutionary acts can be performed only by using language;[12] and even in cases in which an illocutionary act can be performed non-verbally, 'the means for achieving its ends non-verbally must be conventional'.[13] Finally,

---

[8] See L. J. Cohen (1964), pp. 121 ff.

[9] Austin (1962, p. 101.

[10] Which is not to say that any act which has a perlocutionary consequence should be classed as a perlocutionary act (see Chapter 1, Section 2 (i)). For some interesting remarks about perlocutionary acts see Ted Cohen (1973).

[11] Austin (1962), p. 117.

[12] Austin (1962), p. 119.

[13] Austin (1962), p. 118.

Austin notes that whilst an illocutionary verb can replace 'Y' in the schema:

In saying X I was doing Y

a perlocutionary one cannot. But in the schema:

By saying X I was doing Y

'Y' can be replaced by a perlocutionary verb, but not by an illocutionary one.[14]

However, Austin himself concludes that the last test is a slippery one. Moreover, we have already seen grounds for doubting the emphasis which Austin places on the conventionality of the illocutionary act; so we can hardly expect the notion of convention to provide the key to understanding the difference between illocutions and perlocutions. And whilst it is true that described in very general terms perlocutionary acts can be performed by use of non-verbal means, one could not convince someone, for instance, that Searle's criticisms of Austin's theory of speech acts is correct without saying something. Finally, as Austin points out, problems arise because though a perlocution always involves the production of consequences, there are three ways in which an illocutionary act may also do so without thereby becoming a perlocutionary act.

Firstly, Austin claims, to perform an illocutionary act I sometimes have to ensure that my audience understands what I am trying to do. If I fail to do so, then I have failed to secure 'uptake'.[15] But, Austin goes on to argue plausibly enough, in such cases securing uptake is a necessary condition of performing the act, not a consequence of it which may or may not occur, and is thus distinguishable from a perlocutionary effect.

In a second class of cases illocutionary acts have what might be called 'conventional consequences'. If a vicar marries Jack and Jill, then they both acquire the status of a married person, and, as a consequence, each acquires various legal obligations and rights which he or she did not have before. Is the illocutionary act of marrying then also a perlocutionary act because it has such consequences? Austin plainly wishes to answer negatively; but to do so has to invoke an unexplained distinction between 'taking effect' and being a consequence.[16] He would

[14] Austin (1962), Lecture X.
[15] Austin (1962), p. 115.
[16] Austin (1962), p. 116.

have done better perhaps to point out that, as in the first class of cases, these consequences are not ones which may or may not occur, and so differ from standard perlocutionary effects. Indeed, all the examples of perlocutionary acts cited by Austin involve effects specifiable independently of any particular act of which they are the consequence; the effects can also be produced without anyone performing any illocutionary act; and they lend their name to the associated perlocutionary act. But the case under discussion is quite different; it is unclear that the consequences of the marriage are independently specifiable (Jill is now a married woman and Jack a married man, etc.); they cannot be brought about unless some marriage ceremony is gone through; and the effects do not give their name to an associated act.

In a third class of cases Austin points out that an illocutionary act invites a response; if I ask a question I hope for an answer, if I give an order I expect compliance, etc. Doubtless, it is my respondent who answers my question not me, so answering my question is not something that I *do*. But suppose I order a subordinate to buy shares for me and he does so, then it would seem to be true to say that I bought some shares, i.e. that the buying of the shares, which is a consequence of my order, is something which I did. So here, perhaps, is a point at which the distinction between the illocutionary and the perlocutionary is far from clear.

So, whether or not one is sympathetic to Austin's distinctions, it has to be conceded that if illocutionary acts are to be identified by the fact that they can also be perlocutionary acts, and usually involve performing locutionary acts, then it is very unclear what an illocutionary act is. The crucial distinctions between the locutionary and the illocutionary on the one hand, and the illocutionary and the perlocutionary on the other have just not been made clearly and cleanly.

2. AUSTIN'S DISTINCTIONS REVISITED

The distinctions tentatively presented in this section are I believe close to Austin's; but I do not wish to defend them on a ground as tenuous as that. Rather I want to do so because they are defensible in their own right, and have a place in any comprehensive theory of language.

Austin himself thought that the distinction between illocutions and perlocutions was the one 'likeliest to give trouble',[17] but it has proved to be the other way round. Most critics grant that there is some distinction between perlocutions and illocutions, whereas the nature, and indeed the very existence, of the distinction between illocutions and locutions has been fiercely debated. I shall, therefore, consider what by common consent is the least problematical of the distinctions first.

(i) Illocutions and perlocutions

If reporting is an illocutionary act and persuading a perlocutionary one, then the former is certainly not conventional in the way in which marrying is. Non-linguistic conventions no more have to be complied with to give a report than they do to persuade someone. Nevertheless, a language may make available linguistic, and hence conventional, means of indicating what one is doing in the former case, whereas it cannot do so in the latter. Hence, the availability of such an explicit form as 'I report that all is lost.' Not that prefixing 'I report that . . .' to a sentence used to make a report is the only way of indicating that one is giving a report; one could, for instance utter 'This is NN reporting' instead, and then go on to give one's report. The important point is that if an act is an illocutionary one, then there is no reason in principle why some linguistic means of indicating that it is being performed should not exist. Hence, the existence of such means is one important indication of an illocutionary act.

The root idea of a perlocutionary act is of an act which when performed by saying something can be redescribed as the performance of an illocutionary act with certain consequences. So if I persuaded you to go to the Brown's party, then perhaps what I did was to say that they would be disappointed if you did not go, which led you to believe that you ought to go. But though in this sort of case a perlocutionary act can be redescribed as an illocutionary act with a certain sort of consequence, it is difficult to see that an illocutionary act can ever be redescribed as a consequence of a perlocutionary one. Probably Austin was right to argue that being substitutable for 'Y' in the

---

[17] Austin (1962), p. 119.

schema 'By saying X I did Y' is not an infallible mark of a perlocutionary verb. However, if 'X' in the schema:

By X'ing I did Y

is replaced by a perlocutionary verb, an illocutionary verb cannot replace 'Y'; whereas if an illocutionary verb replaces 'X' a perlocutionary one can replace 'Y'. This is not a criterion of course, but it is an important indication of a difference.

In this connection Ted Cohen's claim that a perlocution can be the point of an associated illocution is of interest.[18] Thus, one may state in order to persuade, threaten in order to intimidate, and vote in order to elect. Since one could not, for example, persuade in order to state, then to the previous point that a perlocution can be the consequence of an illocution, but not vice versa, we may add the further point that an illocutionary act may be performed in order to bring about a certain perlocutionary effect, but not vice versa.

Some of the problems that arise from the fact that an illocutionary act can have consequences without thereby becoming a perlocutionary act Austin himself shows how to dispose of.[19] Others disappear if it is remembered that perlocutionary acts are acts, so that whatever is true of acts in general is true of them. Thus, one would not expect that if Jack voluntarily performs an act (e.g. answering a question) in response to an illocutionary act of Jill's, that a description of Jack's act is also one of an act which Jill performed. Quite generally, descriptions of voluntary acts performed by Jack are not descriptions of acts performed by Jill, even if Jill did something which led to Jack doing them; *a fortiori* descriptions of voluntary acts performed by Jack are not descriptions of perlocutionary acts performed by Jill.

Cases in which the response to an illocutionary act is a voluntary action apart, to perform an illocutionary act which has a certain consequence is not necessarily to perform a perlocutionary act. Jack's claim that he is interested only in her mind may convince Jill that he is not interested in that at all; but that is not to say that he convinces her of this, what does is his saying something which is so implausible. Similarly, Jack's remark that the sky is dappled like a mackerel may convince Jill that it will be fine tomorrow, even though he had no intention

---

[18] Ted Cohen (1973), p. 500.
[19] See Chapter 1, Section 1 (ii).

of making her think this, and indeed does not know that a
'mackerel' sky is a sign of good weather. Thus, what Jack says
may convince, even though Jack does not.

This is not the place to attempt a detailed account of convincing; but enough has been said to show that the fact that an
illocutionary act has a consequence, or plays some role in bringing something about, need not mean that it must also be a
perlocutionary act. Whether it is will depend on what actually
produces the consequence, the intentions of the speaker, and
many other things. There is plainly no danger of every illocution—assuming that illocutions can be distinguished from
locutions—becoming a perlocution.

(ii) Locutionary acts and truth values

The notion of reference prompts an interesting question about
the Austinian distinction between locutions and illocutions:
why should he count reference as part of the locutionary act?
After all, to refer is to do something, just as to promise is. A
plausible answer is that Austin does so because if a sentence is a
declarative he counts as part of the locutionary act all, and only
all, that we must know about a person's use of that sentence in
order to be able to determine the truth conditions of his utterance. So that if a proposition is that which is capable of being
true or false, then what determines which locutionary act has
been performed also determines which proposition has been
expressed by the speaker.

This leaves it unclear what is to be said about other sentence
types. However, a possible suggestion about imperatives would
be that one specifies the locutionary act performed by specifying
all that it is necessary to know about a person's use of it to
determine whether a given action would, or would not, conform
to it. And, perhaps, following a familiar proposal, an interrogative can be treated as a special kind of imperative.

On such a view it is not difficult in principle to distinguish a
locutionary from an illocutionary act. For one can surely know
what proposition someone is using a sentence to express without
knowing whether he was stating, suggesting, defining, etc. But
what if a sentence is an explicit performative, e.g. 'I report that
all is lost', and, as some have argued,[20] explicit performatives

[20] See, for instance, Lemmon (1962) and Warnock (1973).

can be true or false? Would not the proposal shipwreck? For, in such cases, it seems that the locutionary act would be identical with the illocutionary act.

An answer would be that if explicit performatives can be true or false, then one would know which locutionary act was performed in the case in question if one knew that the proposition that the speaker reports that the army is in flight has been expressed; but that one would know which illocutionary act, if any, was performed only if one knew that that proposition is true. A different answer is, however, preferable. It rests on the assumption that in any utterance there can be, subject to certain qualifications,[21] only one illocutionary force indicator, and that the remainder of the utterance is meant to have the force indicated. Thus, an utterance of 'I report that all is lost' contains only one force indicator, 'I report that . . .', and the remainder of the sentence uttered is to be understood to be uttered with the force of a report. A reasonable way of applying the account given of locutionary acts to such a case would be to say that one knows which locutionary act has been performed if one knows which proposition the speaker expresses by uttering that part of the sentence which excludes the performative prefix (assuming that the embedded sentence is declarative); and to know which illocutionary act has been performed one must additionally know something about the legitimacy of the speaker's use of the performative prefix. So that even if explicit performatives can be true or false, a distinction between locutionary and illocutionary acts is not ruled out by the view here advocated.

(iii) Austin's sense and reference

Whether this view was Austin's is another matter, and one which cannot be settled definitively since his remarks markedly underdetermine the distinctions he wishes to make. However, the view is plainly consonant with the spirit of the following: 'we can use "meaning" also with reference to illocutionary force—"He meant it as an order"', &c. But I want to distinguish *force* and meaning in the sense in which meaning is equivalent to sense and reference, just as it has become essential to distinguish sense and reference within meaning.'[22] Of course, the

[21] See Chapter 4, Section 5 (iv).
[22] Austin (1962), p. 100.

nature of the contrast intended between force on the one hand and sense and reference on the other is far from clear, since Austin gives no account of what he means by 'sense' and 'reference' in *How To Do Things With Words*. However, he had earlier given a fairly careful account of conventions of reference and conventions of sense as they operate in the simplified models of 'How to Talk',[23] the former being associated with the nominal expressions of the language, the latter with the predicables. Simplified or not, Austin seems to have taken the models of 'How to Talk' seriously, for in the earlier paper 'Truth' analogues of the two sorts of convention are to be found called, respectively, demonstrative and descriptive conventions.[24] The former correlate 'the words (=statements) with the *historic* situations, &c., to be found in the world'; whilst the latter correlate sentences 'with the *types* of situation, thing, event, &c., to be found in the world'. Given an utterance of such a sentence as 'I tell you that John is tall', and Austin's account of truth, the conditions in which the sentence-part 'John is tall' is uttered to say something true are fully determinate. But Austin's account does not tell us what to say about the explicit performative as a whole. Arguably, conventions other than descriptive and demonstrative ones are needed to do this, and certainly this is what Austin himself seems to have thought, since he held that explicit performatives are not true or false.

Be that as it may, it is necessary now to consider two views of the relationship of locutionary to illocutionary acts which are inconsistent with the one which I wish to develop. They are:

(a) That the meaning of a sentence is a function of the illocutionary acts it can be used to perform;[25] and,

(b) That meaning and force are not distinct; or, what amounts to the same thing, a locutionary act is not distinct from an illocutionary one.[26]

It is to the consideration of these that I now turn.

---

[23] Austin (1961), p. 182.
[24] Austin (1961), p. 89.
[25] See Alston (1968).
[26] See L. J. Cohen (1964) and Searle (1968).

CHAPTER 2

I. MEANING AND USE

IF THE range of illocutionary acts a sentence can, uttered literally, be used to perform is called its 'illocutionary act potential', then the theory that a sentence's meaning is a function of its illocutionary act potential can be attributed to Alston.[1] It is, of course, unclear that acceptance of Alston's theory must lead to a denial of the locutionary/illocutionary distinction, since it may be possible to distinguish the illocutionary act potential which a sentence used by a speaker has from the particular illocutionary act he is using it to perform on that occasion. But even so Alston's theory should still be rejected, since it misrepresents the relation between meaning and illocutionary force.

It is not easy to say precisely what Alston's theory is. However, it is clear that he thinks that there is a dependence of meaning on use, for he writes that

in saying what the meaning of an expression is, what we do is not to designate some entity which could be called the meaning of the expression, but rather to exhibit another expression which has some sort of equivalence with the first. . . . It seems plausible to say that it is equivalence in the way they are used that is crucial . . . And this suggests that a meaning-statement is to be tested by examining people's employment of the expressions in question, to determine whether they are employed in the same way.[2]

By a meaning-statement Alston understands a statement of the sort:
  'Procrastinate' means *put things off*
the point of the italics being to indicate that the italicized expression is not being used in the ordinary way, though the statement as a whole carries the presupposition that the hearer understands the italicized expression.

---

[1] See Alston (1968) and (1964).
[2] Alston, (1968), p. 146.

It has been argued[3] that Alston vacillates between trying to give an account of the meaning of expressions, and giving an account of the conditions in which meaning-statements are acceptable. But it seems rather that he thinks that to do the latter thing is to make a definite, though limited, contribution to the former. A definite one, because if we have an acceptable account of the conditions in which a meaning-statement of the form ' "E" means E' is true, then we are in a position to explain what the meaning of 'E' is in any case in which we are in possession of a true meaning-statement about 'E'. But also a limited contribution, because many expressions cannot be the subjects of true meaning-statements, since there are no other expressions (in the same language anyway) which are synonymous with them. Hence, presumably, the importance Alston attaches to developing a theory of word uses which enables one to do for words what we already can do for sentences, namely, say what their use is.[4]

2. INDEPENDENT SPECIFICATIONS OF USE

However, if Alston does not claim to have described a way of specifying the meaning of every expression, he plainly thinks that he has outlined a way of specifying that of some, and the most important of these are sentences. Moreover, it is reasonable to assume that he thinks that the way outlined is an independent way in the very minimum sense that it is not in general necessary to know the meaning of an expression 'E' in order to be able to specify its meaning. Hence, if the meaning of sentences can be specified in the way Alston outlines, then one thing that could be meant by the claim that a sentence's meaning is a function of its use is that there is an independent way of specifying its meaning which involves reference to, or depends on, facts about illocutionary act potential.

There are at least two very different reasons why this might be so:

(a) It might be possible to know that a given sentence x has the same illocutionary act potential as some other sentence x', and additionally to know what x' means without knowing what x means. In that case an independent

---

[3] Attfield and Durrant (1973), p. 284.
[4] Alston (1968), p. 164.

specification of the meaning of x would obviously be possible.

(b) It might be possible to establish what x's illocutionary act potential is, and thus put oneself, given Alston's theory, into a position to specify its meaning, without making use of any knowledge one has of the meaning of it or any other sentence belonging to the same language. This might be so because one was able to specify x's illocutionary act potential directly without reference to its meaning, or to the meaning and use of any other sentence. Or it might be so because as well as being able to know that x has the same use as x' without knowing what x means, one is also able to specify the illocutionary act potential of x' without reference to its meaning, or to that of any other sentence belonging to the language, etc. In either case there would be an independent way of specifying the meaning of x.

It seems to me that if Alston does vacillate it is between (a) and (b). Perhaps he only wishes to maintain (a), or something like it.[5] But many things he says are very suggestive indeed of (b). Why, for instance, regard it as a drawback from the point of view of his theory that we do not have ways of specifying the uses of words comparable to those we have of specifying the uses of sentences?[6] That Alston does think that there is an important difference is clear from the following:

two words have the same use when they are intersubstitutable in a certain way; but this criterion of intersubstitutability does not itself provide us with any characterisation of the use the words both have. With sentences, on the other hand, we have done both these jobs. Two sentences have the same use to the extent that they have the same illocutionary-act potentials; in specifying the illocuotinary acts in question, we have specified the use(s) that each of the sentences has. This can be done for each sentence without bringing in the claim that another sentence has the same use.[7]

That is, because we have a theory of sentence use we can say what a sentence's use is without claiming that some other sentence has the same use; but because we do not have a general

[5] See Cooper (1972), p. 71.
[6] See Alston (1968), p. 164 and Alston (1964), pp. 36 and 38.
[7] Alston (1964), p. 38.

theory of the use of words we cannot do anything analogous for a word. This granted, there seems to be every reason to embrace (b).

Moreover, (a) is of no theoretical interest, whereas (b) is. If (a) were true, but (b) were not, then the explanation of the meaning of a sentence x would always terminate with a sentence x' having the same use as x, but such that it is in principle possible to know what its meaning is without knowing what that of x is. The sentences x and x' would have the same meaning because they have the same use, and one would be able to explain what x means to anyone who knows what x' means. But plainly this goes no way at all to establishing that the meaning of either x or x' is a function of its use; nor does it show how it is, if it is.

3. DETERMINATE AND NON-DETERMINATE UTTERANCES

Clearly, the crucial question posed by (b) is whether it is possible to identify a sentence's illocutionary act potential independently, in the way required. If we call a description of an illocutionary act which does not specify its content a 'short description' (e.g. 'He reported something'), and one which does a 'full description' (e.g. 'He reported that they are late'),[8] it is clear that if the meaning of a sentence does depend on the illocutionary acts it can be used to perform, it is illocutionary acts under a full description which are relevant. 'You are early' and 'You are late' can both be used to state, complain, criticize, etc., yet for all that they do not mean the same.

Consider then a determinate sentence, i.e. one which contains no token-reflexive items, and hence which does not have a different truth value on different occasions of utterance. Ignoring the tense:

(1) Wellington won at Waterloo in 1815

would be such a sentence. However, certain qualifications apart, it is difficult to see how anyone in the position of Quine's jungle linguist, that is, having a language of his own but understanding no English, could independently identify the illocutionary act performed by uttering (1) under a full description.

First the qualifications. It will, of course, be the case that an educated European will almost certainly have heard of both

8 See Holdcroft (1968), p. 173.

Wellington and of Waterloo, so that the names in (1) will be familiar to him. Moreover, knowing that the syntax of English has many similarities with other European languages, our man may be able to make quite a good guess about what is being conveyed by (1). But Quine's jungle linguist is not in this position. He has no prior knowledge of the similarities of the language he is studying to other languages; he knows nothing about the history of the people whose language he is studying; he does not share a common culture, etc. Even more obviously he cannot be supposed to be in possession of information about the speech habits of particular speakers. Thus, he does not know, for there is no one to tell him, that a certain person is in the habit of talking at length about Waterloo. He has to guess at what is being said from clues provided by the context of utterance. These will be such things as objects which are observable in that context; the aims of the speaker, which may be apparent in the light of what he does before he speaks; the reactions of the audience to what is said, etc.[9] But if an utterance is a determinate one then it is unlikely that the persons, places, and events referred to are actually present. And whilst it may be reasonably clear that the speaker desires to impart information, and that his audience is disposed to believe what he says, this in itself provides a very slight ground indeed for supposing that the speaker is saying one thing rather than another.

It might seem that with non-determinate utterances the situation is different. Could not our man tell that his host is trying to invite him to sit down from the sort of gesture he makes when he utters 'Sit down', which provides a good clue to his intentions, and from the reactions of other people present when the utterance is repeated but addressed to them, which provides a good clue to what was meant. It is difficult to deny that he could, and that he could go on to make a reasoned guess that by 'Sit down' the speaker meant 'Sit down'. To deny this, though it has perhaps been done,[10] would be to invite the response that if this were so, then language learning would become an incomprehensible mystery.

---

[9] Jonathan Bennett shows the importance of these last two factors in Bennett (1973), p. 159.
[10] Attfield and Durrant (1973), pp. 291–4. Perhaps I have misunderstood their position; but they refuse to allow that even a greeting is independently identifiable.

But, anyway, the crucial question is not whether someone in the position of Quine's jungle linguist could sometimes do this, but whether in the case of numerous, though not necessarily all, non-determinate utterances he could. For Alston's theory requires that such a person should be able to identify independently the illocutionary act performed under a full description in a large number of such cases. Knowledge so obtained will then form the basis of his knowledge of facts about the meanings of sentences.

Now circumstances which give the jungle linguist a good indication of what illocutionary act under a full description the speaker is performing are, *ex hypothesi*, ones which have to give him a good indication both of the illocutionary act under a *short* description that is being performed, and of the meaning of the sentence. For we arrive at a full description by tacking on to a short one a description of what the speaker meant by the words he uttered, which, assuming literalness of use, will not differ from one of what they mean. But if this is so, then the identification of a sentence's meaning cannot be parasitic on the identification of illocutionary acts under a full description that are performed by uttering it, since any set of circumstances in which one is able to identify an illocutionary act under a full description performed by uttering a sentence is one in which one is already in a position to say what that sentence means.

If this is correct, then it ought to be possible for one to be in a position to formulate a reasonable hypothesis about the meaning of a sentence, and yet be in doubt about the illocutionary force with which it was uttered. Equally, it ought to be possible for one to be in a position to formulate a reasonable hypothesis about the illocutionary act performed under a short description, and yet be unable to formulate one about the meaning of the sentence uttered. For not only can illocutionary acts under a short description and the meaning of sentences uttered vary independently of each other, in that the same act can be performed by different sentences and the same sentence used to perform different acts, but there is no reason why there should not be much better clues on some occasions about sentence meaning than there is about illocutionary force, and vice versa.

In the present context the interesting question is whether it is indeed possible to formulate a reasonable hypothesis about sentence meaning without being able to formulate one about illocutionary force, for if one can, then plainly there can be no logical dependence of sentence meaning on illocutionary acts, even under a full description. Suppose, for instance, that a native points to a fierce-looking striped animal and utters 'Yo Bohu', seemingly unconcerned by the animal's somewhat threatening behaviour. The fact that the animal is a tiger, that it has only just intruded on what has been an unchanging scene, that it occupies a spot where there is nothing else of interest, and that the sentence seems to be of a type used by the natives to identify animals, trees, etc., leads the linguist to translate the native sentence as 'That is a tiger'. But given the native's insouciance, the linguist may be quite unable to decide whether the native is merely informing him that it is a tiger, or, more urgently, warning him that it is. Perhaps the native is really unconcerned by the presence of the tiger, because he believes for one reason or other that there is no threat; but perhaps he is terrified and only appears unconcerned because he believes that he is safe only so long as he does. Nothing in the native's demeanour may enable the linguist to decide between these alternatives; yet for all that he remains rightly confident about his translation of the sentence uttered.

To concede that this is a possible case is to concede that there is no general logical dependence of sentence meaning on illocutionary force. Moreover, there are other difficulties with the view that there is such a dependence. If it were correct, then (a) two sentences with the same meaning ought to have the same illocutionary act potential; and (b) two sentences with the same illocutionary act potential ought to have the same meaning. However, if there are two synonymous expressions 'E' and 'E'', then presumably

'E' means E', and
'E' means E

will mean the same thing, though only the first can be used to explain the meaning of 'E'. As for (b), there is, for instance, no statement which can be made now by uttering 'I am sitting down' which it will not also be possible to make by uttering 'I was sitting down'; but the two sentences do not mean the same.[11]

---

[11] Relativizing illocutionary act potential to a speaker, time, and place would avoid this objection. However, consider the sentences 'I am here' and 'the person

However, even if the thesis that there is a logical dependence of meaning on illocutionary force has to be rejected, it remains possible that Austin's theory is vulnerable simply because it tries to draw a distinction where none can be drawn. Commenting on Wiggins's advocacy of the thesis that to specify a sentence's meaning is to specify its truth conditions, Alston argues that his views are not at odds with such a thesis: 'For the special case where the illocutionary act, a potential for which is in question, is something statemental or assertive, something that is straightforwardly true or false, the conditions imbedded in the rule would coincide with the truth conditions for the statement.'[12] Since the rule in question is one which specifies illocutionary act potential, Alston's thesis suggests not so much that meaning depends on illocutionary force, but that locutionary and illocutionary acts are not distinct. It is this view, the second mentioned at the end of Chapter 1 as an objection in principle to the account of a locutionary act there sketched, which must now be considered.

now uttering this is here'. Is the statement I make by uttering the first always the same as the one I make by uttering the other? It is difficult to tell without knowing whether the two sentences have the same meaning.

[12] Alston (1971), p. 36.

CHAPTER 3

I. DIFFERENT, OR RELATED, DESCRIPTIONS OF THE SAME THING?

CLAIMS THAT what has been construed as a distinction between two different things is only a distinction between different ways of describing the same thing are notoriously perplexing. Often one feels that something has been lost, and that whatever the protestations of non-reductive intent, one set of descriptions is being taken as basic at the expense of the other. On the other hand, a defender of such a contention may sometimes justifiably claim that he has no reductive intentions; consider, for instance, Spinoza's theory of the Mind–Body relation.

What then are we to make of the following claim by Searle? Is it in intention reductionist?

The concepts *locutionary* act and *illocutionary* act are indeed different, just as the concepts *terrier* and *dog* are different. But the conceptual difference is not sufficient to establish a distinction between separate classes of acts, because just as every terrier is a dog, so every locutionary act is an illocutionary act.[1]

The contention that the concepts of a *locutionary* and an *illocutionary* act are different suggests that descriptions employing the former cannot be eliminated in favour of ones which employ the latter—as is the case with the pair, said to be analogous, *terrier* and *dog*. On the other hand, Searle recommends that the concept of a *locutionary* act should be dispensed with, which is hardly a sensible recommendation unless the descriptions making use of it can be dispensed with without loss. So there is an apparent hiatus.

However, consideration of Searle's conception of a locutionary act shows, I think, that the second alternative is his preferred one. For a description of a locutionary act is for him a description of the 'sense' and 'reference' with which the words of a sentence are uttered, *including its performative prefix* (or other

[1] Searle (1968), p. 413.

indicator of illocutionary force) if it has one; and because, in his view, every sentence contains some indicator of illocutionary force, every such description is a description of an illocutionary act. Hence, his claim that the study of illocutionary acts is not in principle distinct from one of the meaning of expressions; each leads to the other. In *Speech Acts* he concentrates on trying to show how rules for meaningful expressions can be abstracted from language-independent characterizations of illocutionary acts; but, if he is right, one ought also in principle to be able to move in the opposite direction.

2. SEARLE'S MAIN THESES[2]

Searle's basic hypothesis is that speaking a language is a rule-governed activity, and this resolves itself into two constituent hypotheses:

[firstly] that speaking a language is performing speech acts, acts such as making statements, giving commands, asking questions, making promises, and so on; and more abstractly, acts such as referring and predicating; and, secondly, that these acts are in general made possible by and are performed in accordance with certain rules for the use of linguistic elements.[3]

The second constituent hypothesis is, however, most implausible. The possibility of performing such acts as warning and threatening hardly depends on the existence of the performative prefixes 'I warn that . . .' and 'I threaten that . . .'. It would surely be extraordinary if speakers of a language which did not contain these prefixes could neither warn nor threaten because it did not. Austin's speculation that in a 'primitive' language the difference between a warning, information, and a prediction is not marked, and that 'explicitly distinguishing the different *forces* that an utterance might have is a later achievement of language, and a considerable one'[4] is *a priori* linguistics, but plausible for all that. Moreover, it does reflect the important truth that the performance of some illocutionary acts does not

---

[2] In this discussion I use 'locutionary' in the way in which Searle does, and not in that advocated in Chapter 1, because I think his arguments can be met in the terms in which it is stated. The principal difference is that he counts the sense and reference of a performative prefix as part of the locutionary act, whereas I do not.

[3] Searle (1969), p. 16.

[4] Austin (1962), p. 72.

presuppose the existence of explicit linguistic ways of indicating that they are being performed.

However, plausible or not, Searle's contention is that to speak a language is to perform rule-governed acts. Hence, his contention that though it might seem that a study of such acts is a study of *parole* rather than of *langue*, this is not so because any adequate study of speech acts *is* a study of langue.[5] This he argues follows from the so-called 'Principle of Expressibility':

PE For any meaning X and any speaker S whenever S means ... X then it is possible that there is some expression E such that E is an exact expression of or formulation of X.[6]

Given PE, the conclusion (C.1) that a study of speech acts is also one of sentence meanings follows, Searle argues, because:

A.1 just as it is part of our notion of the meaning of a sentence that a literal utterance of that sentence with that meaning in a certain context would be the performance of a particular speech act, so it is part of our notion of a speech act that there is a possible sentence (or sentences) the utterance of which in a certain context would in virtue of its (or their) meaning constitute a performance of that speech act.[7]

However, it is arguable, to say the least, whether every sentence is uniquely related to a particular determinate illocutionary act. Ignoring for a moment the context of utterance, such a sentence as 'Leave me alone' plainly stands in a one–many relation to the determinate acts of ordering, begging, requesting, etc., to be left alone which it can be used literally to perform.[8] Of course, given a sufficiently determinate context of utterance, then a literal utterance of the sentence can be correlated with a determinate speech act, namely, the one that was performed by uttering it in such a context. But this is hardly surprising if we count as part of a context—as Searle seems to do—any factor constitutive of an illocutionary act. For in that case the claim boils down to the truism that if a context C contains those factors

---

[5] Searle (1969), p. 17.
[7] Searle (1969), p. 20.
[6] Searle (1969), p. 17.
[8] On a different interpretation 'Leave me alone' would be correlated with non-determinate acts of ordering, begging, requesting, etc., instead of with determinate acts of ordering someone to leave one alone, begging someone to leave one alone, etc.

which make the literal utterance of a sentence an illocutionary act of kind K, then to utter a sentence in that context will be to perform an act of kind K. So, for example, to utter 'Leave me alone' in circumstances which make the utterance an order is to order someone to leave one alone. Clearly, however, this truistic statement describes a complex relationship between the utterance of a sentence, a context of utterance, and the performance of an act; and it is not possible in the absence of the reference to context to pair the sentence uniquely with a determinate act.

Be that as it may, it will be urged that the crucial question posed by Searle's procedure is not whether each sentence can be paired uniquely with a determinate speech act, but whether each determinate speech act can be paired uniquely with a possible sentence. The natural suggestion to make at this point is that a determinate illocutionary act of kind K can be paired with a possible sentence x provided that there are circumstances C in which a literal utterance of x would constitute the performance of an act of kind K. But if this suggestion is adopted, it turns out that there is not a one–one correlation between determinate illocutionary acts and possible sentences. For instance, if we take the relevant context to be one in which an utterance of a sentence is an order, then the determinate act of ordering that I be left alone can be paired with both of the sentences 'Leave me alone' and 'I order you to leave me alone', and these are certainly not synonymous.

It might seem that there is an easy way of producing a one–one correlation, namely, to associate with a particular determinate speech act that possible sentence (or class of synonymous sentences) which can, in an appropriate context, be used literally to perform the act in a fully explicit way. Hence, 'I order you to leave me alone' would be correlated with the act of my ordering you to leave me alone, but 'Leave me alone' would not. A particular version of PE which Searle appeals to on occasions is relevant in this context, namely:[9]

PE′ If by uttering a sentence x a speaker S V'd ('V' ranges over illocutionary acts), then it is in principle possible for S to utter a sentence which explicitly indicates that this is what he is doing.

[9] Searle (1968), p. 415.

For if this is true, then to each determinate speech act there corresponds a possible sentence which could in principle be uttered, and whose utterance would, in appropriate circumstances, constitute the performance of the act in a completely explicit way. The force of 'in principle' is difficult to assess, since Searle certainly does not wish to claim that at any given time in a given language the means to perform an act in a completely explicit way already exist.[10] So a possible sentence is not necessarily one which, as things are, could be uttered, since it may be one which could be uttered only if the language were changed in certain respects. But, anyway, PE′ is false. I can, for instance, hint that I am thinking of the Queen, but there is no possible sentence which can be used to perform this act in a fully explicit way. Obviously, 'I hint that I am thinking of the Queen' cannot, since to tell someone that one is hinting that p is not to hint that p, as I argue at greater length in Chapter 4, Section 3 (i). And, whilst it is possible to hint this by uttering the sentence 'She likes horses' (and, of course, countless others), an utterance of this sentence can hardly constitute the performance of the act in a fully explicit way.

A further conclusion which is related to C.1 and which Searle claims also follows from PE is:

> C.2 [we can] equate rules for performing speech acts with rules for uttering certain linguistic devices, since for any possible speech act there is a possible linguistic element the meaning of which (given the context of utterance) is sufficient to determine that its literal utterance is an utterance of precisely that speech act.[11]

And the way in which Searle goes on to develop his theory in detail is fully consonant with C.2. He firstly states a set of necessary and sufficient conditions which have to be satisfied to perform a given speech act, e.g. promising, and then extracts from them semantic rules for the use of a linguistic device whose function is to indicate that an utterance is a speech act of that kind, e.g. 'I promise'.

Undoubtedly, if PE were correct, and both C.1 and C.2 followed from it, then the distinction between locutionary and illocutionary acts would be extremely questionable. However,

---

[10] See Searle (1969), p. 20.
[11] Ibid.

the argument (A.1) designed to show why C.1 follows from PE is very dubious, since it fails to establish that there is a one–one correlation between a determinate speech act and a set of synonymous sentences; and if C.1 is not proven, then the closely related thesis C.2 must also be doubtful. It will be of interest, therefore, to consider Searle's other objections to the Austinian distinction, and the positive merits of the sort of explanation of meaning that he gives.

3. SEARLE *contra* AUSTIN

In an extended criticism of Austin's distinction[12] Searle argues that if it rests on the possibility that the same sentence can be uttered on different occasions with the same sense and reference, but to perform different illocutionary acts, then it cannot be completely general.[13] The meaning of an explicit performative, such as 'I order you to leave', determines the illocutionary force of utterances of itself. So this sentence cannot be used on different occasions with the same sense and reference to perform different illocutionary acts. It is possible, of course, that on some occasions it is used to give an order, but that it is not on others because the speaker lacks the authority on some occasions which he has on others. But to account for this all that we need, according to Searle, is the distinction between attempting and successfully performing an illocutionary act. There is no need to invoke the locutionary/illocutionary distinction.[14]

Now admittedly in some cases the two distinctions coincide; but this is not always so. Locutionary acts, even when characterized in Searle's way, are not always attempts at illocutionary acts;[15] jokes, for instance, can have a serious point, and involve locutionary acts. Further, not all attempts at an illocutionary act result in a locutionary act, some result only in verbiage. Admittedly, even if the distinction between attempting and performing an illocutionary act is not the same as that between a locutionary and an illocutionary act, Searle is clearly right to insist that there is a close connection between aspects of the

---

[12] See Searle (1968); this is discussed at length in Holdcroft (1974).

[13] Searle (1968), p. 407.

[14] Searle (1968), p. 409.

[15] A point which Searle notes (ibid.); but oddly he seems to count it as a further criticism of Austin.

meaning of an explicit performative and the force of utterances of it.

However, he goes on to claim, much more debatedly, that a similar claim can be made about non-performatives. Indeed, he argues that every sentence is force determining, so that it is impossible to describe a locution without describing an illocution. Noting that Austin sometimes uses *oratia recta* to report a locutionary act and sometimes *oratia obliqua*, he asks whether Austin is consistent in doing so, and concludes that he is. For, Searle maintains, an *oratia recta* report of such an act, for instance:

R.1 He said 'Shoot her' meaning 'Shoot her' by it, and referring by 'her' to Sally.

determines the *oratia obliqua* report:

R.2 He told me to shoot her.

Moreover, the latter contains a verb of illocutionary force ('told me to'), so that R.2, which is determined by R.1, is a report of an illocutionary act. The reason why this is so, Searle concludes, is that 'no sentence is completely force neutral. Every sentence has some illocutionary force potential, if only of a very broad kind, built into its meaning.'[16] So every specification of a locution is also one of an illocution.

But how, one might ask, is the very general illocutionary force potential 'built into' the meaning of an imperative related to the specific illocutionary acts that can be performed by uttering it? Searle seems to think that the relation is like that between genus and species, so that in the case in question 'tell (one to)' is the generic verb, and 'order', 'insist', 'request', etc., the specific ones. However, 'tell (one to)' is plainly insufficiently general to qualify as the generic verb. Maybe, to order someone to do something is to tell him to do it. But to dare him to do it is not to tell him to do it, any more than to request him to do so is to tell him to do so. Moreover, it is difficult to see what suggestion would fare better.

It is difficult too to see how there could be a genus/species relationship of the sort Searle envisages for indicatives, i.e., such that,

(a) The potentiality for performing the generic act is possessed by a sentence in virtue of the fact that it is of a

[16] Searle (1968), p. 412.

certain grammatical type, namely, an indicative:
and,

(b) All other illocutionary acts performable by literally uttering a sentence of that type involve performing the
generic act.

Perhaps the most plausible candidate would be asserting. But
though, for instance, hinting may involve asserting, it is not a
specific way of asserting, what is hinted is not asserted, and
neither is what is suggested. Estimating is not asserting; and,
sometimes anyway, neither is ruling, since what is ruled to be so
is so only in virtue of the ruling.

So though there are important facts which Searle draws
attention to in a misleading way, most notably, that the meaning of a sentence partially determines its uses, he fails to establish that every sentence contains an illocutionary force indicator,
albeit of a very general kind. Also, even if he had established
this, it would underwrite a much more modest conclusion than
the first part of A.1, which we criticized earlier, is designed to
underwrite. According to this,

A.1a it is part of our notion of the meaning of a sentence that
a literal utterance of that sentence with that meaning
in a certain context would be the performance of a
particular speech act.

But if non-performatives contain only very general indicators of
illocutionary force, but can be used to perform specific illocutionary acts, then there will be a gap between an account of
their meaning and one of the many different specific illocutionary acts that can be performed by uttering them.

In Searle (1968), Searle seems to argue that this raises no
difficulty of principle if PE is granted: 'it is only a special case
of the distinction between literal meaning and intended meaning, between what the sentence means and what the speaker
means in its utterance.'[17] But if the aim is to show that a sentence's meaning does fully determine the illocutionary force of
utterances of itself, this use of PE is quite illegitimate. For to
show this one has to show not that there always *could* be a sentence x' the meaning of which completely determines the illocutionary force with which a given sentence x was uttered, but that
x's own meaning determines that force.

[17] Searle (1968), p. 413.

Yet a further indication that the claim C.1 that a study of speech acts is also one of sentence meanings is defective would be the breakdown of the sort of explanation of meaning which Searle envisages; and that it does break down I try to establish in the next two sections.

4. THE ROUTE FROM SPEECH ACTS TO MEANING

As pointed out earlier, Searle's programme involves two steps: firstly, describing the conditions that have to be satisfied to perform a particular speech act, e.g. promising; and, secondly, abstracting from these conditions the rules for the use of a particular illocutionary force indicating device. Mention must now be made of a third step which involves attaching these rules to particular items in a particular language, e.g. the English prefix 'I promise . . .', or the French 'Je promets . . .'. There is indeed only one passage in which Searle mentions this third step, and in this he speculates whether the rules attach to items in deep or surface structure.[18] But, anyway, it is clear that he is committed to it.

A crucial question concerns the justification of the move from a premiss of the form (a), 'The rules for the use of a promising device are . . .', to a conclusion of the form (b), 'One meaning of "I promise" in English is . . .'. The obvious suggestion is that one meaning of 'I promise' is to be related to the rules in question provided that one of its literal uses involves conformity with them; the point of the reference to a literal use being to rule out deviant or eccentric ones. But if such a reference is necessary, then it is difficult to conceive of the step from (a) to (b) as one which takes one from premises which are not about items in a particular language to a conclusion which is. For to take the step, information about the literalness (and, hence, the meaning) of a particular item is required.

It is difficult to be sure whether the reference to a literal use is really necessary. But it is clear that if it can be dispensed with Searle gives no hint how this might be done. An investigation of the use of 'I promise' would naturally lead one to investigate its use in sentences, for if it is a promising device, then it ought to be possible to use sentences in which it occurs to promise. Hence, it is natural to turn to Searle's account of the conditions

[18] Searle (1969), p. 64.

that must be satisfied if a sentence is to be used to make a promise.[19] However, a reference to a literal use is actually built explicitly into this account. Nor would it seem that Searle can dispense with it given his amended Gricean theory of meaning, one of the main points of which is that the effect which the speaker intends to produce in the hearer must be intended to be produced by means of recognition of the rules governing the use of the expression uttered. This would seem to mean that a speaker must believe that the sentence he utters is rule-governed, and that he is making an appropriate use of it, i.e. a literal one.

There are other problems too. Firstly, it is unclear whether different expressions have to be synonymous to be promising devices; could not the italicized portion of each of the following be said to be a promising device?

I promise to be there.

I regard myself honour bound to be there.

Scout's honour, I'll be there.

So must not an account of what it is for something to be a promising device be something less than an account of the meaning of particular promising devices?

Connectedly, Searle's account seems to associate with linguistic items sets of conditions which can hardly be directly associated in their entirety with the meanings of those items. Thus, he lists the following rules for a stating device:[20]

Preparatory	(i)	S has evidence (reasons, etc.) for the truth of p.
	(ii)	It is not obvious to both S and H (the hearer) that H knows (does not need to be reminded of, etc.) p
Sincerity		S believes p.
Essential		Counts as an undertaking that p represents an actual state of affairs.

But of these only the essential condition is a necessary condition of stating; an insincere statement, for instance, is still a statement. So, as a matter of urgency, some account of the way in which irrelevant members of this set are to be 'filtered out' to give an account of the meaning of 'state' is needed.

---

[19] Searle (1969), p. 57.
[20] Searle (1969), p. 66.

5. THE SCOPE OF SEARLE'S ACCOUNT

It seems, therefore, that Searle has succeeded at best in describing what conditions linguistic items must satisfy to play such roles as that of a promise-indicator, statement-indicator, etc. But even if he has done more than this and shown how to describe the meaning of such items, nothing considered so far shows how to do this for linguistic items of other types.

It is clear, however, that Searle intends to say something about other types of item. Hence, his contention that an illocutionary act is of the form '$F(p)$', 'F' being replaceable by illocutionary force indicating devices, and 'p' by expressions which express propositions. He further maintains that just as one can perform an act by uttering '$F(p)$' (an illocutionary act), one can also perform one by uttering 'p', which he calls a 'propositional' act. This, in turn, can be analysed into an act of predicating and an act of referring, and it is by an analysis of these that Searle clearly hopes to be able to illuminate various features of referring and predicating expressions respectively.

Indeed, a similar three-step procedure to that already described is repeated in each case, and similar difficulties emerge in an even clearer form. Given Searle's account of reference, for instance, it is unclear that one can move from a premiss of the form (c), 'The rules for the use of a referring expression are . . .', to a conclusion of the form (d), 'E is a referring expression in English', without making use of information about the meaning of E, particularly since one of the rules specifies that one must know whether E contains an identifying description.[21] Hence, it is very difficult to see how conclusions about the *meaning* of E could be derived from a premiss of the form (c) (assuming that the rules are Searle's) in a way that is not question-begging. The inescapable conclusion seems to be that what we have at best is an account of the conditions which must be satisfied for an expression to be a referring expression. Nothing whatsoever is said about the meaning of particular referring expressions.

There are similar difficulties with Searle's account of predication; so that not only does he fail to describe a way of attaching meaning to referring expressions and predicates, but it is difficult to see how the procedure he envisages could do

---

[21] See Searle (1969), p. 95.

this. Thus, the claim that to study speech acts is to study meanings from another point of view is false if taken to be the claim that the meaning of each significant item within a sentence can be explained in terms of the speech acts it can be used to perform. If, however, all that is claimed is that the meaning of some items, notably force indicators, can be explained in terms of the speech acts which the sentences they are part of can be used to perform, then the claim is much less controversial, though, of course much less interesting.[22] It would be hardly surprising if an account of stating turned out to be relevant to the meaning of an expression whose role is to indicate that the speaker is stating. But that would no more justify the claim that meaning can quite generally be explained in terms of speech acts, than the fact that one has to mention parts of the body to explain the meaning of 'walk' justifies the claim that meaning can quite generally be explained by referring to parts of the body.

6. RETROSPECT

The most serious threat to the tentative conception of a locutionary act developed at the end of Chapter 1 is posed by the claim that any attempt to develop a concept of a locution as distinct from an illocution is doomed to failure, since there is in principle no such distinction to be drawn. We can, I think, now claim to have disposed of this threat in the terms in which it was stated; and if Searle fails to show that locutions and illocutions can be equated employing his conception of a locutionary act, we can be fairly sure that they cannot if my conception is employed. However, it is difficult not to sympathize with Searle's view that there must be some connection between the meaning of a sentence and the illocutionary acts that can be performed by one who uses it literally and seriously. Surely, the relation cannot be perfectly arbitrary; if it were, the problem of an audience deciding what use a speaker had made of a sentence on a given occasion of utterance would be insoluble. Thus, though we rejected the explanation Searle offers why an imperative (used literally, etc.) can be used to perform the range

[22] See Warnock (1971) for an interesting discussion of a number of different ways in which it might be claimed that meaning and illocutionary force are connected.

of acts that it can be used to perform, it must be acknowledged that it is plausible to suppose that some such explanation can be given. It is appropriate now, therefore, to turn to consider a different sort of explanation.

CHAPTER 4

I. THE PERFORMATIVE ANALYSIS OF INDICATIVES

THE UNDERLYING structure proposed for such a sentence as:
   (1) John runs.
has often been:

(A)

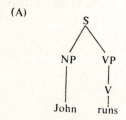

However, Ross has argued (J. R. Ross (1970)) that this is incorrect, and has proposed instead what might be called a 'performative analysis' ('PA' hereafter) of (1), according to which its deep structure is:

(B)

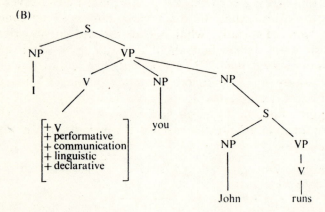

The surface structure of (1), which it is assumed is represented by (A), is then obtained by the performative deletion rule, the effect of which is to delete the highest clause of (B). This proposal about (1), incidentally, is meant to be viewed as 'only one fragment of a far more inclusive analysis which postulates that every deep structure contains only one performative sentence as its highest clause'.[1]

The interest of the proposal for syntactic theory is plain. But it is also of great interest in connection with the question that arises if we grant, as we did in Chapter 3, that a serious and literal utterance of a sentence can have only a limited range of illocutionary forces. For the crucial question then is why is it that a given sentence can be uttered literally to perform some illocutionary acts but not others?[2] In outline, the answer PA gives to this question is clear, namely, that the range of illocutionary acts performable by a literal utterance of, for instance, (1) is in some way delimited by the performative sentence it contains in underlying structure.

The main aim of this chapter is to consider this answer in detail; but before doing so I would like to comment briefly on Ross's arguments for PA.

2. ROSS'S ARGUMENTS

The arguments which Ross presents are syntactic;[3] seven of them are designed to establish that an indicative like (1) has a higher subject; three to establish that the main verb of the higher sentence is a verb like 'say', i.e. a performative verb; and three to establish that the main verb must have an indirect object 'you'. Typically, what one of the arguments tries to establish is that some fact about an indicative which needs explaining is explained if PA is adopted. The cumulative effect of the arguments is, therefore, to establish that PA has very considerable explanatory force, since a wide range of often seemingly unrelated facts can be explained by it. If, therefore, the arguments all hold, the case for PA is undoubtedly a very strong one.

---

[1] J. R. Ross (1970), p. 261.

[2] See Barry Richards (1971).

[3] For additional arguments, primarily of a syntactic nature, for PA see Fillimore (1972), George Lakoff (1972), sec. IV, Robin Lakoff (1969), and McCawley (1968). George Lakoff develops arguments of a semantic and pragmatic kind for PA in George Lakoff (1974), and makes a number of interesting comments about Lewis's proposals in Lewis (1972).

However, it seems clear that many are defective. Indeed, quite a number fail for the interesting reason that the phenomenon to be explained can be found in explicit performatives as well as in simple indicatives. So, even if an indicative with certain features which require explanation has the same underlying structure as an explicit performative, this cannot explain why it has these features, since an explanation why the explicit performative has them is also needed. Presumably, one would not wish to posit an underlying structure for the explicit performative in which it is embedded in yet another performative; and, anyway, to do so would be contrary to the hypothesis that simple indicatives and explicit performatives can have the same underlying structure.

The point is a familiar one, so one illustration should suffice.[4] In 2.1.3, Ross presents an argument which makes a number of points about 'as for' phrases. Reflexives can occur in these when the phrase is prefixed to an embedded clause, as in:

(2) Glinda knows that as for herself she won't be invited.

But there are restrictions on the occurrence of such reflexives. These are, Ross argues, that the reflexive be coreferential with the subject of the next higher sentence. This granted, PA readily explains why 'myself', but not 'himself', can occur in 'as for' phrases prefixed to simple indicatives, as in:

(3) As for myself, I won't be invited.

However, the stated restriction is too severe. The coreferential NP need not be a subject, for if (2) is acceptable, then surely so is:

(4) I told Glinda that as for herself it was too late, but that the others still had time.

More seriously, it seems that 'as for' phrases can prefix explicit performatives, as in:

(5) As for myself, I promise to be there.

Nor is this an isolated case, as a consideration of such verbs as 'state', 'vote', and 'nominate' shows. In 4.2, Ross discusses this case, and acknowledges the difficulties it poses for his analysis. He suggests, however, that perhaps the difficulty is only apparent, and that this is so because the 'for myself' phrase does not

---

[4] See Anderson (1971), p. 21; and Fraser (1971), p. 9. I am greatly indebted to both of these discussions which show that similar counter-examples can be given to many other of Ross's arguments.

modify the performative verb in underlying structure, but is a constituent of the embedded clause. Hence, (5) comes from:

(6) I promise that, as for myself, I will be there.

by use of a preposition rule. In support of this Ross points out that the strangeness of:

(7)* As for me, Tom will be there.

is preserved in:

(8)* I promise you that, as for me, Tom will be there.

So that if reflexivization is applied to (8), and the 'as for' phrase is then preposed, the result, (9), retains the strangeness of (8):

(9)* As for myself, I promise you that Tom will be there.

Thus, the oddity of (9) can be explained in terms of that of (7).

But it is not generally true that the oddity of an explicit performative which has an 'as for myself' phrase in an embedded clause is preserved when the phrase modifies the performative verb, as the following pairs show:

(10)*a** I bet you that, as for myself, he will win.

    a′ As for myself, I bet you that he will win.

    b* I warn you, that as for myself, it will explode.

    b′ As for myself, I warn you that it will explode.

And there surely are cases in which 'as for myself' phrases can occur with explicit performatives, but could not have their origin in an embedded clause, for example:

(11) As for myself, I nominate Smith.

    As for myself, I apologize for hitting you.[5]

So, it seems that 'as for myself' phrases can and do occur with explicit performatives in a way which precludes PA from explaining facts about their occurrence in simple indicatives, since the same sort of question is raised by their occurrence in explicit performatives as is raised by their occurrence in simple indicatives.

Similar difficulties can be raised with many other of Ross's arguments. Further, even if the arguments for the existence of a higher verb succeed, they do not establish that it is a performative verb, only that it is one with the features (+communication), (+linguistic), and (+declarative), so that 'shout' and 'cable' qualify. Hence, even if what Ross calls the 'pragmatic analysis',[6] which permits reference to certain elements in

---

[5] See Anderson (1971), p. 9.

[6] J. R. Ross (1970), p. 259.

the speech act situation, so that there is, as it were, an 'I' and a 'you' 'in the air', was not a serious rival to PA, the case for PA on syntactic grounds would not seem to be very compelling.

3. OTHER ARGUMENTS FOR THE PERFORMATIVE ANALYSIS

Even so it is far from clear that PA should be rejected, since it can be plausibly argued that there are strong arguments for it of a different kind. In particular, it might well be urged that PA goes a long way to explaining how the possible illocutionary forces of a sentence, used literally, are determined by its meaning, and so, in effect, tells us how an illocutionary act depends on, or is determined by, a locutionary one. The proposal made by PA is, of course, that the possible illocutionary forces of a sentence are determined by the performative verb in its highest clause. This clause is not deleted in the case of an explicit performative, though in the case of a simple indicative it is, but otherwise there is no significant difference.

Clearly, this claim made for PA is an extremely far-reaching one. If it is correct, then there seems to be no reason why a theory of formal semantics should not also be a theory of language uses. Thus, on the view in question, semantics threatens to swallow pragmatics. This has been clearly seen by George Lakoff who, in a footnote comment on a point he urges in favour of PA, writes: 'What we have done is to largely, if not entirely eliminate pragmatics, reducing it to garden variety semantics.'[7] However, the impressiveness of this claim should not be allowed to conceal the fact that in some respects it is not very precise. In particular, what could be meant by the claim that the meaning of a sentence determines the illocutionary forces of utterances of itself? Indeed, is it even true? Consider then the following:

IF (1) The meaning of a sentence x so determines the range R of illocutionary forces of utterances of itself that any speaker S who utters x necessarily performs an act belonging to R.

This clearly will not do. Which act S performs is at best only partially determined by the meaning of the sentence he utters. For it is difficult to see how the meaning(s) a sentence has could,

[7] George Lakoff (1972), p. 655.

on a given occasion, have any bearing at all on the illocutionary force of an utterance of itself unless there is some connection between one of its meanings and what S *means* by it.[8] The most obviously relevant connection that there could be is that involved in a literal use. To say that S's use of x is a literal one is to say that there is a meaning M which is one of the meanings of x, and that S means M by x. But I think it likely that there are other relevant connections. A sarcastic utterance of 'That is a *large* helping you have left me' has of course the feature that what S means by his sentence (namely, 'That is a small helping you have left me') is not one of its meanings. However, it seems probable that the range of acts which S can perform by uttering his sentence sarcastically is systematically related to the range that he could have performed by uttering it literally. For instance, the sentence in question used literally might well be used to make an *assertion* and express one's thanks, whereas used sarcastically it might be used to make an *assertion* with a critical intent; so that either way an assertion is involved. However, in the present context it will suffice if we concentrate on literal uses, since the aim is, primarily, to show that there can be a systematic connection between the meaning of the sentence uttered and the range of acts that can be performed by uttering it, and not to trace all such connections.

Plainly, though, the insertion of a reference to a literal use would not itself suffice to make IF (1) acceptable. A literal use does not guarantee an illocutionary act; not only must S's use of his sentence be literal, but he must mean something by uttering it. Kaufman when asked by his bridge partner how he would have played a hand which his partner had just lost replied 'Under an assumed name'. There is no reason not to take his words literally; but he did not mean by uttering them that he would have played the hand under a pseudonym. He was joking, and though his joke had a serious point, he was not actually saying something.

Finally, someone may fail to perform an illocutionary act even though he means something by uttering the sentence he does utter, because, for instance, he lacks the requisite authority. Thus, IF (1) should, at least, be amended as follows:

---

[8] In Grice's terminology this would be S's utterance-type-occasion-meaning. See Grice (1969), p. 148.

IF (2) The meaning of a sentence *x* so determines the range *R* of illocutionary forces of utterances of itself that any speaker *S* who utters *x* literally, and means something by uttering it, will, if he succeeds in performing any act at all, perform one which belongs to *R*.

In essence, the case for IF (2) is that if it were not true, then one could on a given occasion utter a sentence literally to perform any illocutionary act whatsoever.[9] If this were so, then the task of an audience trying to work out which act had been performed on a given occasion might well seem impossible. A speaker who utters a sentence literally, and means something by uttering it, intends the literal meaning of the sentence uttered to provide a vital clue to what he meant by uttering it. It is in this way that sentence meanings are exploited systematically by speakers to enable their audiences to grasp what they mean by uttering their sentences (their utterance occasion meaning in Grice's terminology[10]). It would be very odd indeed if the meaning of a sentence, which was an important determinant of what the speaker meant by uttering it, in no way determined the illocutionary force of the speaker's utterance. For if that was the case then it would be possible that though what a speaker meant by uttering 'The king is dead' literally is that the king is dead, he nevertheless asked a question.

Now if IF (2) is correct, then the crucial questions become: what is the value of *R* for a given sentence? And, how does that sentence's meaning determine that value? To these questions advocates of PA who maintain that any performative verb whatsoever can occur in underlying structure would, I think, reply that a particular sentence's range *R* will be restricted to that illocutionary act named by the performative verb in its highest clause in underlying structure, and those other illocutionary acts which one has to perform to perform it. So that according to this thesis (which I'll call the 'strong thesis'), if '*V*' (e.g. 'warn') is the highest performative verb in *x*'s underlying structure, and '*V*'' (e.g. 'state') the name of an illocutionary act which one has to perform to perform that named by '*V*', then both '*V*' and '*V*'' name acts belonging to the range of illocutionary acts determined by the meaning of '*x*'.

[9] For a detailed argument see Barry Richards (1971), p. 527.
[10] Grice (1969), p. 148.

But one can imagine a more modest answer. Suppose that an advocate of PA maintains that in those cases in which the highest clause is deleted, the performative verb in that clause can only be a very general verb, one like 'say', but not one like 'predict', 'report', or 'concede'; then he might suggest that a particular sentence's range will be restricted to that illocutionary act which is named by the verb in its highest clause, and those other illocutionary acts to perform which is to perform it. So, according to what I shall call the 'weak thesis', if 'V' (e.g. 'state') is the highest performative verb in x's underlying structure, and if 'V'' (e.g. 'concede') is the name of an illocutionary act to perform which one has to perform the one named by 'V', then both 'V' and 'V'' name acts belonging to the range R of illocutionary acts determined by the meaning of x. Whereas R will be rather restricted on the strong thesis, since if I am predicting, then, perhaps, I must also be stating, but I certainly am not also reporting, announcing, or informing, etc., it will be much less restricted on the weak thesis. For example, the sentence:

(12) They are going to charge.

can be used to predict, warn, announce, tell, inform, etc., and since doing each of these things plausibly involves saying something, then according to the weak thesis all of these acts would belong to R in the case of (12).

Of the two theses the strong one is much the more interesting, since it alone purports to explain why a particular utterance of a sentence has the *specific* illocutionary force that it has. The weak thesis is incapacitated from doing this, in the vast majority of cases anyway, by the much weaker restriction which it places on R. I shall, therefore, concentrate discussion on the strong thesis. But, firstly, I want to try to show that whilst the weak thesis does draw attention to some important insights, they are not ones which give aid or comfort to PA. If I succeed, I will incidentally have provided a further reason for concentrating attention on the strong thesis.

4. THE WEAK THESIS

(i) We have, in effect, already discussed and rejected a version of the weak thesis. Searle's claim that 'I tell (you to)' is part of the meaning of every imperative, and that the meaning of this verb is related like that of genus to species to the meanings of such verbs as 'order' and 'request' which name specific acts which can be performed by uttering an imperative, is a version of the weak thesis.[11] Searle's particular proposal fails, because if I am begging, pleading, or even requesting, then I can hardly be said to be telling anyone to do anything. It is, moreover, difficult to see how any other proposal would fare better which satisfies the conditions:

(a) that the potentiality for performing the generic act is possessed by a sentence in virtue of the fact that it is an imperative; and

(b) all other illocutionary acts performable by uttering an imperative involve performing that act.

Clearly, an enormous variety of different specific acts can be performed by uttering an imperative. Some, like commanding, require compliance by the person commanded; others, like advising, do not, for whether you take my advice is up to you. Some are primarily directed towards the interests of the person to whom the command is addressed, e.g. warning, and advising; but others, such as ordering, requesting, and pleading, are not. So it seems very unlikely that there is a meaning element common to each one of 'command', 'order', 'advice', 'counsel', 'warn', 'insist', 'request', 'beg', and 'plead'.

(ii) However, it does seem reasonable to suppose that the fact that a sentence is of a certain grammatical type does place some restriction on the range of illocutionary acts which can be performed by uttering it literally. If all that I know about the sentence you uttered is that it is an indicative, that it was uttered literally, and that you meant something by it, then the presumption is that whatever you were doing you were not questioning, pleading, or commanding.

On the other hand, the range within which the act you performed could fall is a very extensive one, since it could belong to any one of three of the major classes of illocutionary act proposed by Austin in the final chapter of *How To Do Things With Words*, namely, expositives, verdictives, and behabitives. This remains true if for the rather rough and ready scheme proposed by Austin the much more refined one proposed by Vendler in Chapter 2 of *Res Cogitans* is substituted. Interestingly, Vendler argues that grammatical distinctions underlie Austin's

[11] See Chapter 3, Section 3.

distinctions, and that performative verbs belonging to different classes have different sorts of nominalized sentences as their objects. In outline the detail of Vendler's theory is summarized below:

(a) *Expositives* ($N_i V$ that $NV+$)

state	concede	guess
contend	deny	suggest
maintain	postulate	confess
insist	remind	testify

(b) *Verdictives* ($N_i V N_j$ (as) N /A)

rank	place
grade	appraise
call	define
rule	analyse

(c) *Commissives* ($N_i V$ to $V+$)

promise	refuse
guarantee	decline

(d) *Exercitives* ($N_i V N_j$ to $V+$)

order	beg
request	dare

(e) *Operatives* ($N_i V N_j$ to be (come) N_k)

appoint	ordain
confirm	condemn

(f) *Behabitives* ($N_i V N_j$ P nom (past $(V+)$)))

thank	apologize
congratulate	criticize

(g) *Interrogatives* ($N_i V$ wh-nom (N V+))

ask	inquire
question	

Some of Vendler's claims are disputable; but he is surely correct to associate indicatives intimately with expositives, verdictives, and behabitives. So it should not be surprising that there are sentences, such as 'He is first', which can be used to state (a class (a) act), or to rank (which is from class (b)), or to congratulate (which is from (f)). Of course, 'He is first' may not be a typical indicative in this respect. The sentence 'There will be no plastic in A.D. 2000' cannot easily be imagined being used to perform an act from class (f). But even if it cannot, it would not constitute a counterexample to the thesis being argued for, which is:

(13) If a speaker S utters an indicative x literally and means something by uttering it, then if he succeeds in performing an illocutionary act it will belong to one of the classes (a), (b), or (f).

The existence of indicatives whose utterances can belong to some, but not all, of these classes does not falsify this.

But may it not be that, weak though it is, (13) is too strong? For by uttering an indicative one can supply someone with a practical reason for doing something, and sometimes when this is so it might seem that one can be said to perform an act belonging to (d). Thus, for instance, an important person's utterance of 'The door is open' might, it could be argued, be classed as an order if it was uttered with the intention of getting the door closed.

However, if possible cases of this kind are considered in detail it is doubtful whether they are genuine counterexamples to (13). Suppose, for instance, that the person to whom the remark is addressed is responsible for seeing that the door is kept shut. Then the point of uttering 'The door is open' may be to remind him of his responsibility, and thus get him to discharge it. But in that case there is no counterexample to (13), since reminding is a class (a) act. Suppose, to take a different case, that the speaker utters the sentence with a perfectly normal intonation, leaving his audience to work out for itself what he hopes to achieve by making his statement. In that case it would seem to be most natural to say that he is hinting; and since hinting is a class (a) act, albeit of a special kind, there is, once again, no counterexample to (13). Suppose, finally that the speaker utters the sentence with some special intonation, or emphasis, hoping thereby to make it clear that he means by it 'Shut the door.' Then, since his use of the sentence is not a literal one, (13) is not falsified, since it is a claim about *literal* uses of indicatives. Assuming then that this review of possible types of case is exhaustive, (13) is indeed very plausible. But if it is true, can a rationale of the claim it makes be found?

Rejecting the version of the weak thesis meant to satisfy (a) and (b) of Chapter 4, Section 4 (i) which posits an occurrence of 'say' in the underlying structure of each indicative, but accepting the claim that sentence-type is a determinant of illocutionary force, the obvious thing to do is to look for something else to do the job which the generic verb of illocutionary force was meant to do. Hare has recently made a suggestion:

Any complete explanation of the meaning of a verb occurring in a sentence must explain the meaning of its mood (in the sense in which indicative and imperative are moods) as well as, for example, its tense, person, voice, and so forth; and it is hard to see how this could be done so otherwise than by specifying the kind of speech act to which that mood is assigned by the conventions which constitute our language. To be in a certain mood is to be assigned to the performance of a certain genus of speech acts.[12]

Presumably, the suggestion is not that the mood is itself related as genus to species to a set of speech acts, but rather that it is related to the genus as a whole, so that an indicative mood indicator could not have a reading like 'say'––a conclusion which is surely correct. Nevertheless, Hare sees a close connection between the indicative mood and assertion, for he says that the meaning of 'is' in the indicative mood can be explained 'by reference to the speech act of assertion'. Hence, his claim: 'We know [the meaning attached to the indicative mood of the verb 'is'] when we know that it is the mood used for the speech act of asserting, and not, for example, commanding', which suggests that an indicative mood indicator has the reading 'can be used to assert', or 'is assertible'.

But how would the supposition that every indicative contains a mood indicator with this reading explain (13)? It would appear to do so, if at all, only because if a sentence is assertible, then uses of it can be true or false. Clearly, the most general restriction on a sentence which can be used literally to perform acts belonging to the classes (a), (b), or (f), is that it be capable of expressing something true or false, unless, of course, an explicit performative is used, in which case this restriction applies to the embedded clause.[13] This is not to say that all of these acts involve a claim that something is true or false. But the connection between expositives and truth or falsity is clear. For if someone asserts, suggests, or conjectures something, he asserts, suggests, or conjectures that it is true; and to understand what a person conjectures or suggests by uttering a sentence x, one must have a grasp of the truth conditions of x just as much as one does to understand what he asserts by uttering x. Arguably, the expression of some verdicts is not, strictly speaking, true or false. But since they are meant to be correct, it is hardly surprising

---

[12] Hare (1970), p. 7.
[13] Without prejudice to the question whether the performative 'as a whole' is true or false.

that they are expressed by sentences that can express something
true or false; and one could not understand what verdict was
being conveyed by utterance of a sentence *x* unless one knew its
truth conditions. Behabitives are a heteregeneous lot; but, at
least, when a sentence is used to express an attitude (e.g.
approval), or feeling (e.g. sympathy), or to compliment or
criticize, what is being approved of, sympathized with, compli-
mented or criticized is always something that is believed to have
happened. Hence, the appropriateness of a sentence which can
express something true or false in these cases also.

Why not then suppose that the function of the indicative
mood indicator is to indicate or show that a sentence which
contains it has truth conditions? Such a theory is obviously as
general as the theory that the indicative mood indicator has the
interpretation 'is assertible', for whatever, used literally, is
assertible has truth conditions, and assertibility has to be explained in terms of truth and falsity rather than vice versa.
Moreover, since an adequate semantic theory will have to
specify the truth conditions of indicatives, what an indicative
mood indicator will indicate on this account is something which
has to be specified anyway. So this is a more economical theory,
and one, moreover, which does seem to explain (13). Finally
and gratifyingly, the theory neatly fits in with the account of a
locutionary act sketched in Chapter 1. According to this, to
know what locutionary act was performed on a given occasion
by the literal utterance of an indicative *x*, we need to know what
the truth conditions of the speaker's utterance are. Since the use
of *x* is a literal one, these will be determined by those of *x*; and it
will be possible to use the locution, in virtue of the fact that it
has truth conditions, to perform those acts which can be performed by the literal utterance of *x*.

So we have an account of one, admittedly rather minimal,
way in which a sentence's meaning restricts the range of illocutionary acts that can be performed by uttering it. But it is not
an account which lends either aid or comfort to PA. For, apart
from growing out of a rejection of the weak thesis which posits
an occurrence of 'say' in the underlying structure of each indicative, what it in turn posits, a mood indicator, is not an
illocutionary, or indeed any other sort of verb.

What then of the strong thesis?

5. THE STRONG THESIS

(i) There is no reason to suppose that (13) is the only truth about *R* in the case of indicatives; 'The bull charged the man' can, for instance, hardly be used to predict because of its past tense. Clearly, factors other than mood indicators can determine the force potential of an indicative, so that there is no objection in principle to the strong thesis.

Insofar as there is a principal objection to it, it is that the role which a performative prefix plays in an explicit performative is one which it is difficult to see a deleted clause playing. The following sections will be devoted to preparing the ground for this objection, and in the course of doing so a number of other objections will be considered, beginning with a rather assorted lot.

(ii) *One and only one?* According to PA a sentence has one and only one performative verb in its highest clause. But, as Fraser has pointed out, there seem to be numerous counterexamples to the claim that the performative verb must be in the highest clause. Consider the following:[14]

(14) *a* I am pleased to be able to offer you the job.
      b I would like to congratulate you.
      c I see that I must concede that he has lost.
      d You will be astonished by the fact that I apologize for being late.

Utterance of these can constitute respectively, an offer, congratulations, a concession, and an apology, though in no case would the verb seem to be in the highest clause. Of course, if this is so, PA (in its strong version) requires modification rather than abandonment. But the modification needed might be considerable, particularly if the next point, also due to Fraser, is considered as well. This questions the requirement that a sentence can have only one performative verb.

The clearest cases in which this is violated are conjunctions, such as the following:

(15) *a* I accept that the government had to do something, but deny that it had to do that.
      b I deny that I bit him, but admit that I kicked him.
      c I warn you that he is dangerous, but ask you to see him.

14 The first two examples are Fraser's; see Fraser (1971), p. 2.

The utterance of the first sentence of the conjunction in each case is clearly meant to have a different force from that of the second. But in no case does the first performative verb dominate the second, or vice versa, so it does not determine the force of the utterance as a whole. Hence, if anything did, it would have to be some other performative verb. But what could it be? And what could its role be, since the utterance as a whole surely has no force to be determined, distinct from that which its conjoined constituents separately have?

Another interesting type of case which Fraser mentions involves appositive relative clauses. Consider the following: .

(16) *a* I deny that the accused, who has now lost his job, is a communist.

b Tell Bill, who now has a phone, that I shall be late.

c Where did Jane, who gave me this, live?

Utterance of these would consitute respectively a denial, a request, and a question, but the content of the relative clause is not respectively denied, requested, and questioned, so that in each case the force of the relative clause is distinct from that of the utterance as a whole. In each of the examples the relative clause has assertoric force, but this is not necessary in view of the following:

(17) *a* Mary, whom I promise to introduce you to, is beautiful.

b Mary, whom I dare you to give this to, is over there.

There is, admittedly, nothing specially surprising about these examples. There is no reason why the conjunction sign in a grammatically complex sentence (e.g.) (15) *a* should not sometimes be used to mark the conjunction of distinct utterances, so that to utter that sentence is to issue more than one utterance. The principle, one sentence, *ergo*, one utterance is not logically compelling. And since a sentence containing an appositive relative clause is logically equivalent to a conjunction, why should it not sometimes be possible to issue more than one utterance by uttering such a sentence? Nevertheless, there are a number of questions to be asked. Why is it not usual to mark the assertive force of the relative clauses in (16) *a–b* by use of a performative prefix? Is this because though there is one in underlying structure, it is compulsorily deleted; or is it because one does not occur in underlying structure at all? If the latter alternative obtains then illocutionary force does not always depend on the presence of a performative verb in underlying structure. Secondly, it would seem possible for a restrictive relative clause to have assertoric force, even though an utterance of the sentence to which it belongs does not: e.g. 'Is the girl I kissed last night John's sister?' Such cases would seem to present knottier problems,[15] as do such sentences as:

(18) *a* I order you to tell him that it is raining.

    b I ask you to remind him that he promised to see me.

Perhaps, however, all of these problems could be solved by modifying the strong thesis; and whether or not they can, the difficulties urged to date all involve complex sentences, so that as a thesis about simple sentences it remains unshaken. The arguments of the following sections are, therefore, important, since they apply to simple sentences.

(iii) *Implicit and explicit forms.* It has often been noted that there are illocutionary acts which cannot be performed by uttering an explicit performative. For example, I can hint that you are living above your means, though there is no explicit performative I can use to do this. To utter:

(19)* I hint that you are living above your means.

would not be to hint.

The problem posed for the strong thesis by the existence of such acts is clear. There is, presumably some reason why the explicit form is odd, or unacceptable. This may be such that it follows that the performative verb in question (e.g. 'hint') could not occur in underlying structure as a performative verb, any more than it can in surface structure; or it may follow that even if it could occur in underlying structure, its presence could not explain why a sentence with that underlying structure could be used to perform the act in question (e.g. to hint). Either way, the force of an utterance of the sentence could not depend on the presence of a given performative verb in underlying structure. And if this could be so in a number of cases, why should it not be so in all?

For example, it would seem that what precludes the use of (19) to hint that you are living above your means is the principle that what is hinted at must not be adverted to openly. This

---

[15] The main one being that we cannot 'split' this into a conjunction of an utterance of 'I kissed a girl' and one of 'Is a girl John's sister?'; cf. Vendler (1968), p. 13.

should not be confused with the different, and indeed mistaken claim that to hint one must intend to conceal the fact that this is what one is trying to do. Hinting is not, like insinuating, an essentially covert act; but it does involve the use of indirect means, so that the audience has to work out for itself what it is the speaker is hinting. The speaker may provide very broad hints indeed that *p*, but if he really is hinting that *p* he must not give the game away entirely by uttering 'I hint that *p*.' Thus, if I want to hint that Wagner wrote *Das Rheingold* in 1862, then I am not going to utter the sentence.

(20) I hint that Wagner wrote *Das Rheingold* in 1862.

for to utter it is not to hint. If on the other hand, having asked who wrote what famous opera in 1862, I actually give a hint by providing a clue, e.g.:

(21) It was the first of a set of four.

then use of the explicit form is also precluded, since I am not hinting that it is the first of a set of four operas, but that it is *Das Rheingold*.

Hinting is one of a group of acts which might be called 'indirect' illocutionary acts, all of which satisfy the condition:[16]

(22) If a sentence is used literally to perform an act of this kind, then there is standardly a discrepancy between something which the speaker *S* intends to convey by uttering *x*, and that which he says or states.

So, for instance, someone who hints that Wagner wrote *Das Rheingold* by uttering (21) literally says only that the opera was the first of four, but he intends to convey more than that. Other members of the group would be intimating, and suggesting; arguably, implying could be added, though even if it could, the group would remain a small one.

The fact that the group is a small one might lead someone to urge that the existence of indirect speech acts does not pose much of a threat to the strong thesis, since they are a marginal phenomenon. Why the fact that they are few in number diminishes their value as counterexamples needs, of course, to be explained. But the objection misses the point anyway, since the feature, noted in the case of (21), that a sentence can be used to perform a given act, though its corresponding explicit form

---

[16] For more detailed discussion, see Holdcroft (1975).

cannot is not confined to indirect speech acts. Suppose that by uttering:

(23) I was unavoidably detained, and do hope that I haven't held things up.

I was apologizing for being late; then I cannot make it clear that this is what I am doing by prefixing 'I apologize' to my sentence, since I am not apologizing for being unavoidably detained. Similarly, I can agree that Smith was an outstanding student by uttering 'His student essays were worth publishing', or illustrate his quality by uttering 'He read all major texts in their original language', but the corresponding explicit performatives could.not be used to do these things.

Now, presumably, even if (21) is used to hint that Wagner wrote *Das Rheingold* in 1862, it cannot have the underlying structure:

(21') I hint that it was the first of a set of four.

for precisely the same reason which prevents (21') itself being used to hint that Wagner wrote *Das Rheingold* in 1862. Indeed, if the strong thesis were correct, then (21) would sometimes have to have two performative verbs in underlying structure, 'say' and 'hint', since it is sometimes used both to say something and to hint, though sometimes it would need to have only one, i.e. when it is used only to say something. One of these, 'say', would, presumably always be present, and would have (21) as its object; the other, 'hint', would, however, only be present on some occasions, and what its object would be is quite unclear.

Thus, the existence of indirect speech acts, and of such acts as agreeing, illustrating, and explaining, constitutes a very serious problem for the strong thesis. However, the arguments used throughout this section have taken it for granted that the function of a performative prefix is to indicate that the sentence to which it is attached is being used to perform a certain sort of illocutionary act, and perhaps this assumption is not sound.

(iv) *Force indicating.* Whatever the function of a performative prefix is, it is clear that it does not express a truth condition of the sentence to which it is attached.[17] Someone who utters 'I

---

[17] This does not, of course, exclude the possibility of a paratactic analysis; nor does it rule out the possibility that explicit performatives 'as a whole' are true or false.

assert that Jill is there' to assert that Jill is there does not assert something which is true only if it is true that he asserts it. What he asserts is in no way different from what he would have asserted had he uttered 'Jill is there' instead to make his assertion, namely, that Jill is there.

Some might agree that the same thing would be asserted by uttering the two sentences, but urge that what would be asserted is not that Jill is there, but that the speaker asserts that she is. However, it is plain that this view has many unacceptable consequences. If it were correct, then p would be tantamount to (i.e. would have the same truth conditions as) 'I assert that p.' So it would be something of a mystery to know how anyone could ever assert plain p, since attempts to do so would always constitute the different assertion that the speaker asserts that p. And since a person nearly always does succeed in asserting what he tries to assert, the ratio of true assertions to false ones would be vastly different, on the view in question, from what it is. Indeed, the difficult thing to do would be to say something false.

The function of a performative prefix must, therefore, be either to describe, or to indicate, the force with which the attached sentence is uttered. There is no need, of course, to oppose description to indication, but there is some reason to stress the indicatory role of a performative prefix. The supposition that it has one would help to explain why, for instance, it can occur parenthetically, so that the following are only stylistic variants:

(24) *a* I warn you that Jill is there.
      b Jill, I warn you, is there.
      c Jill is there, I warn you.

For if it is indicating something about the use of an attached sentence, then, being logically independent of it, in the nature of a comment, the prefix might be expected to have considerable freedom of occurrence. The supposition also helps to explain why the possible concatenations of performative prefixes are very restricted, in a way in which concatenations of verbs of propositional attitude are not. Thus, though the following are strained:

(25) *a* I know that I believe that I fear that I want to kill my aunt.

b I hope that I am surprised that I doubt her.

they are construable. However, concatenations of performative prefixes of comparable complexity are not. Often something of the form:

$$(26) \quad I \left\{ \begin{array}{l} \text{declare} \\ \text{state} \\ \text{announce} \end{array} \right\} \text{that I } V$$

(in which '*V*' stands for an illocutionary act) is possible, but it seems to be only a rhetorical flourish equivalent to the plain 'I *V*'. Ignoring these cases, construable combinations of performative prefixes of anything like the complexity of (26) are hard to find. Fraser proposes the following:[18]

(27) *a* I admit that I concede the election.

 b I announce that I hereby promise to be timely.

 c I insist that I dare you to leave now.

But *c* seems very dubious; *b* clearly conforms to the pattern of (26); and, so it seems, does *a*. It is, of course, not surprising that examples are difficult to find, if a performative prefix has a force indicating role. For if it has, then there should be few construable concatenations of prefixes, since everything within the scope of an initial force indicator would have to be understood to be part of what is being uttered with the indicated force, and is hence precluded from having a force indicating role itself.

It is difficult, however, to see how, if a prefix does have a force indicating role, one which has been deleted can perform this role unless it is possible to tell that it has been deleted. It is reasonable to suppose, therefore, that the strong version is committed to the view that the clause deleted by the performative deletion rule is always recoverable, so that one can always know as much about a sentence's underlying form as one needs to tell with what force it has been uttered. But it is doubtful whether this condition on recoverability is generally satisfied. Certainly, the performative deletion rule does not seem to satisfy the condition on recoverability suggested by Katz and Postal, and by Kimball.[19] What is deleted is not identical with another item in the sentence; nor is it one of a fixed list of items which figures in the structure index of the deletion rule.

---

[18] Fraser (1971), p. 4.

[19] Katz and Postal (1964), p. 81; Kimball (1973), p. 48.

There are a number of problems connected with this one. The strong thesis maintains that the deleted verb is a specific verb. But what is that verb in the case of 'He is first'? 'Assert' because I can assert that you are first? But then why not 'announce', or 'place', or 'congratulate', on the grounds that the sentence can be used to perform each of the acts named by these verbs? There seems to be no good reason to prefer any one suggestion to any other. It might be proposed, I suppose, that which verb is present depends on the way in which it is being used, but such a proposal would lead to rather a dramatic, and otherwise unmotivated, increase in the number of underlying structures.

This sort of difficulty is even more severe with imperatives. Consider the following:

(28) *a* Shut the door.　　　　*a'* I order you to shut the door.
　　　b Come to bed.　　　　　*b'* I beg you to come to bed.
　　　c Give it up.　　　　　　*c'* I advise you to give it up.
　　　d Hold your breath.　　　*d'* I suggest that you hold your breath.

If we suppose that the structure underlying *a* contains 'order', then the structure underlying *a'* underlies *a* also. But why should the verb underlying *a* be 'order'? If it is, then the use of *a* to beg, advise, or suggest becomes puzzling in the extreme. Indeed, since each of *a–d* can be used to order, beg, advise, and suggest, there is no more reason to suppose that a structure containing 'order' underlies each of them, than there is to suppose that one containing 'beg', or 'advise', or 'suggest' does. Anyway, since if PA were true, the context would have to indicate an appropriate performative prefix, and this in turn an illocutionary force, it would seem to be much simpler to conclude that the context indicates an illocutionary force.

It might be urged that the foregoing argument unduly simplifies, since it ignores the possibility that the fact that one specific verb has been deleted rather than another might be indicated by, for example, the presence of a modal auxiliary, such as the 'may' of permission in 'You may go', whose presence might plausibly be held to relate the sentence to 'I give you permission to go.' An interesting suggestion of this kind is that made by Robin Lakoff (1969), who argues that facts about the distribution of 'some' and 'any' can be accounted for by adopting a version of PA. However, Fraser would seem to have shown

that 'the distribution of *some* and *any* does not appear to correlate in any systematic way with promises and threats . . .',[20]
though Robin Lakoff's arguments require that they
do.

Still, it would be foolish to deny that there are cases in which
the presence of a morpheme, or of a particular form of a morpheme, is a strong indication that an utterance of a sentence
would have a specific illocutionary force. However, to grant
this would not be to take back anything that was said, for
example, about (28) *a–d*, for these sentences surely do not contain anything which could play this role.

6. WEAK OR STRONG?

We have been investigating the answer given by PA to the
question why it is that a given sentence, used literally, can be
used to perform some illocutionary acts but not others. The
answer which PA gives to this question, it will be recalled, is
that the range of acts performable by a literal utterance of a
sentence is delimited by the performative verb it contains in
underlying structure. According to one version of the theory,
the weak thesis, only a limited range of performative verbs can
occur in underlying structure. But according to another version,
the strong thesis, any performative verb whatsoever can so
occur; and this makes the strong thesis much the more interesting one, since it alone is in principle capable of accounting for
the specific illocutionary forces with which sentences are uttered.

Unfortunately, the case against the strong thesis is formidable.
It raises problems for the deletion rule. There seem to be a large
number of possible candidates for the role of underlying verb
for a sentence such as 'They are going to charge', with no obvious reason to prefer one to another. Moreover, if it is proposed
that what verb is present depends on what the use of the sentence is, then the objection is that this seems to multiply the
number of underlying structures alarmingly. There are also
ways of using sentences which are such that to indicate that one
is using a sentence in this way would not be so to use it; and
there are sentences which can be used to perform illocutionary
acts in certain indirect ways which raise similar problems.

[20] Fraser (1971), p. 18.

Finally, and most importantly, a performative prefix has a role which it is difficult to see a deleted clause playing.

If, for these reasons, the strong thesis is rejected, as it should be, then we are left with the weak thesis. But though this points in the direction of something which is acceptable, it too, as we have seen, has to be rejected.

CHAPTER 5

ONE OF the conclusions of Chapter 4 was that the range of uses of an indicative is partially determined by the fact that it is in the indicative mood, and that for a sentence to be in the indicative mood is not for it to contain a very general performative verb, but for it to have truth conditions. The important question now is whether it is possible to reach similar conclusions about other sentence-types, of which the most important are imperatives and interrogatives. If it can be shown that it is, then this would be a striking confirmation of the conclusion reached about indicatives, since it would be to show that it is one which can be generalized in a significant way. Further, the way would then be open to giving an account of the connection between meaning and use which both explains how a sentence's meaning partially restricts the range of its uses, and leaves room for the particular intentions with which it was uttered on a particular occasion, together with various features of the context of utterance, to determine which act within that range was performed.

I. ALLEGED DIFFERENCES BETWEEN INDICATIVES AND IMPERATIVES

Assuming that the widely expressed view that interrogatives are, in effect, a special kind of imperative is true, then attention can be focused on imperatives which, at first sight, seem to be strikingly different from indicatives in a number of respects. What can be asserted by uttering an indicative need not have been asserted by any one to be true or false, and something can be believed to be true even though it has not been asserted to be true. However, if obedience and disobedience stand to commands as do truth and falsity to assertions, then it is difficult to see that an analogous series of remarks can be made about commands. For there can be no question of obedience or disobedience unless a command has been given by someone. What can be commanded by uttering an imperative must have been commanded by someone before it can be either obeyed or disobeyed. So commands do not seem to be detachable from their authors in the way in which assertions are.

However, if the notions of obedience and disobedience, which are at home only with a limited range of acts such as ordering, are replaced by the more neutral notions of conformity and nonconformity, and 'command' is interpreted as 'what is or can be commanded', on the model of 'statement' interpreted as 'what is or can be stated', then there seems to be no reason why commands, pleas, and the like should not be considered in independence from their relationship to their authors, as statements are. Thus, one could say what conformity and nonconformity to a 'command' consisted in even though it had never been issued. If this seems objectionable, then a hypothetical way of putting things could readily be adopted, i.e. one could speak of what it would be to conform if the command were issued.

Since commands, pleas, and the like are always commands to someone to do something, there are prima facie two very different ways of viewing them, one from the speaker's point of view, and one from that of the person who is commanded. Viewed in the former way the emphasis will be on what the speaker does, e.g. according to some, indicate certain wishes that he has. Viewed in the latter it will, of course, be on what the person commanded has to do to comply. If similar conclusions to those reached about indicatives can be established about imperatives, then the latter point of view must be the more important one, and I aim to show that it is. However, the other point of view has seemed very attractive to many others, and I want to try to show first that it is not in fact a genuine alternative to the one I advocate. I shall also discuss a number of important issues raised by Hare's analysis of imperatives, before attempting to spell out my own positive position in Chapter 6. This chapter is, therefore, something in the nature of an extended interlude.

2. EXPRESSING THE WILL OF THE SPEAKER

It seems reasonable to maintain that part, anyway, of the speaker's aim when he utters an imperative is to draw his audience's attention to the fact that he (the speaker) wants it to do something.[1] Hence, the attractiveness of Katz and Postal's suggestion, which seems to have been the first of its kind, that the underlying structure of an imperative contains a morpheme *I* which has the reading 'the speaker requests (asks, demands, insists etc.) that' (which they abbreviate to RIM).[2] This suggestion is somewhat qualified in a footnote where they say that 'Actually the meaning appears to be what is common to the readings of this list of verbs.'[3] However, they do not say in further detail what they have in mind—although it could be that it is the view, discussed and rejected in Chapter 3 that the verbs all name specific forms of a generic act to which there corresponds a generic verb, and that it is the meaning of this generic verb which they have in common.

They offer two sorts of argument in support of their analysis: semantic and syntactic. The main arguments of the latter kind are that certain sentence adverbs (e.g. 'certainly', 'possibly') and negative preverbs (e.g. 'hardly', 'scarcely') cannot occur with imperatives, and that certain verbs (e.g. 'hope', 'want') cannot occur in imperatives though they can occur in the corresponding indicative sentences of the form 'You will . . .'. So, 'Postulation of an imperative morpheme permits these selections to be stated in the phrase structure in terms of co-occurrence restrictions on *I*, and sentence adverbials, preverbs, subclasses of verbs, etc.'[4] Assuming that these arguments succeed, they certainly point to the need to find some way of stating these restrictions, and positing an element like *I* would be one way of doing this. But the arguments do not require that the element posited has the interpretation which Katz and Postal suggest *I* has. At most they point to the need to posit some element on which the selection restrictions can be stated. The other set of arguments are, therefore, of special interest, since they relate directly to the question of the interpretation of *I*.

---

[1] Cf. A. Gardiner (1951), p. 310: 'Neither alternative, however, does justice to the most salient feature of all the sentences there united by a common label, namely, the speaker's desire for an action not dependent solely on his will. This is the true differentia of requests. . . .' Whilst in D. A. J. Richards (1971), p. 18, we read: 'the imperative mood . . . is a form in the language, typically intended to be used, and understood to be used, to communicate a person's own intention about another's actions, where there is some context which typically makes these intentions effective.'

[2] Katz and Postal (1964), p. 76.

[3] Katz and Postal (1964), p. 49.

[4] Katz and Postal (1964), p. 78.

The first of these is that the supposition that I has the suggested interpretation accounts for the paraphrase relations between:

(1)   *a*   I request you go home.

      b   You go home.

      c   Go home.[5]

However, it is not clear that there is any need to maintain that there is a paraphrase relation between (1) *a* and (1) *b* just because by uttering (1) *b* one can request someone to go; and Katz and Postal's qualification of their initial suggestion about the interpretation of I threatens to undercut their argument anyway. For whatever meaning, if any, is common to the meaning of 'request', 'demand', 'insist', etc., it is difficult to see how if I had that meaning there could be a paraphrase relation between (1) *a* and (1) *b*.

Another argument is that the supposition that I has the suggested reading accounts for the fact that the following are anomalous:

(2)   *a**   believe the claim

      b*   understand the answer

      c*   want more money

      d*   hope it rains

For the corresponding sentences of the form 'I request that you . . .' are also anomalous, and the reason why they are is 'due to the fact that part of the meaning of "request" makes it anomalous to request someone to do something which he cannot wilfully choose to do.'[6] So if the existence of I with the interpretation suggested is posited in underlying structure, it is easy to account for the anomalous character of (2) *a–d*.

Undoubtedly, this is a partial explanation—partial in that the question remains why sentences of the form 'I request that . . .' are anomalous. But other explanations of the anomalous character of (2) *a–d* would seem to be possible. Alternative interpretations of I apart, it seems likely that the fact that the verbs in question are all stative is relevant.[7] Katz and Postal would presumably argue that it is not, since they cite 'Know

---

[5] Katz and Postal (1964), p. 76.

[6] Katz and Postal (1964), p. 77.

[7] Stative verbs are illuminatingly contrasted with activity, accomplishment, and achievement verbs by Zeno Vendler in his paper 'Verbs and Times': see Vendler (1967).

your lesson' as an imperative. But should not the injunction be to learn one's lesson, that is, to read and study the work prescribed? If it is done properly, this will, indeed, result in your knowing things which you do not yet know; but if the injunction is to have a point, there has to be something one can do to acquire that knowledge, and it is this that one is enjoined to do.

Thus, though there is a case for positing an item like *I*, it is far from clear what its interpretation should be. Katz and Postal's suggestion certainly has explanatory merits. However, it is difficult to see how the supposition that *I* has as specific a reading as 'The speaker requests . . .' can be squared with the fact that an imperative can be used to order, insist, advise, and demand as well as to request. On the other hand, it is extremely unlikely that *I* could have so general an interpretation that its reading could be part of that of each of 'request', 'order', 'insist', 'advise', 'demand', etc.

The dimension of the problems involved in this last supposition can be gauged from a more extensive survey of the illocutionary acts that can be performed by uttering an imperative than the somewhat cursory ones we have undertaken so far, consisting merely of lists of contrasting acts. Now some illocutionary acts performable by uttering an imperative serve, or are intended to, the interests of the person addressed, e.g. warning, recommending, and advising. A solicitor's duty, for instance, is to look after your legal interests, and to advise you accordingly. Other acts, however, are often not performed to forward an interest of the addressee; threats, requests, and commands, for instance. It is true, of course, that it may be in the general interest that commands are complied with, so that it may be in the addressee's interest to comply for that reason. But, even so, it is unlikely that a particular command is given to forward a particular interest of the addressee. Further, whilst some acts performable by uttering an imperative are distinguished by the fact that the speaker is in a position to sanction the addressee, or is in a position of authority over him, so that the speaker can compel compliance, in many other cases this is not so. In these cases whether the addressee does comply will depend either on his willingness to help the speaker even though doing so does not benefit him (i.e. the addressee), or else on his sense of self-interest and self-preservation. Thus, someone may comply with

your request in order to help you, though the person who benefits is you, not him; whilst if he heeds your warning, then the
calamity that is avoided is one which would have involved him
not you. Since these contrasts vary independently, a fourfold
classification is possible:[8]

	Hearer Interested	Not Hearer Interested
Sanctioned/ Authoritive	(a) warn[9] counsel authorize	(b) command order direct forbid insist instruct
Not-Sanctioned or Authoritive	(c) warn counsel advise suggest recommend dare permit authorize	(d) request ask entreat beg pray

Now, some imperatives (e.g. 'Give it to me') can be used to
perform acts belonging to each of these categories. So that if *I*
is to have an interpretation which is part of the meaning of
every verb in each category, or is, at least, consistent with each
of the meanings, it is difficult to see what it could be other than
one designed to mark the fact that conformity and nonconformity are the appropriate responses.

3. SOME ALTERNATIVES

(i) It might be urged that the basic trouble with the proposal
of Katz and Postal is that the reading proposed for *I* is the same
as that for a specific performative verb, and that the way out of

---

[8] For a more elaborate account to which I am indebted see Alf Ross (1968), p. 60.

[9] 'If you go on like this, I'll have to sack you', assuming that it is not in your interest to be sacked, is an example.

the impasse is to propose a 'psychological' interpretation according to which *I* has the reading 'The speaker intends . . .', or the reading 'The speaker wants . . .' But these suggestions will not do either.

Consider the first. Is it even true that someone issuing a command must intend it to be complied with? Dummett argues that it is not:

> the utterance of a sentence of a certain form, unless special circumstances divest this act of its usual significance, in itself constitutes the giving of a command. It is irrelevant what intentions the person speaking may have had: it is, for instance, possible to give a command in the hope that it will be disobeyed, and that one will therefore have an excuse for punishing the person commanded; or again, one may simply be carrying out the duty of transmitting the orders given by a superior.[10]

It is difficult to accept that the speaker's intentions are always totally irrelevant. Persons in authority do not always choose to exercise it, so, at the very least, the question whether, on a given occasion, the speaker intends to exercise his authority can arise. However, Dummett is surely right to point out that a command may be given in the hope that it will be disobeyed. Whether this refutes the proposal under consideration, though, depends on how it is interpreted. If the proposal is that

(3) Shut the door.

is equivalent to:

(4) I intend you to shut the door.

then Dummett's objection is decisive, for the command can be in force even though it is false that the commander intends compliance. But the proposal is pretty implausible anyway. Commands are not simply statements of intention; to announce my intention to marry Jill is one thing, to command that the marriage takes place another. It is desirable, therefore, to interpret the proposal differently, if this is possible. One suggestion would be that though (3) is not equivalent to (4), an utterance of (3) conventionally counts as an indication that the commander intends the door to be shut, in a similar way to that in which a greeting conventionally counts as an indication that the speaker is pleased to see a certain person, but is not a statement

10 Dummett (1973), p. 301.

to that effect. Dummett's point would seem to be less decisive against this suggestion, for the fact that the sadistic commander does not have the conventionally indicated intention would not mean that his utterance did not count as a conventional indication that he did have it. Still, even on this interpretation, to give a command, and then to follow it with the remark that one did not intend, or want, it to be fulfilled, ought to be something a speaker could not intelligibly do, since to do so would be to deny the existence of the very intention which the command is a conventional indication of. Yet, surely, this can be done; the official doing his job may make it clear that he certainly does not want you to comply with his command, or is at least indifferent whether you do, but add that he has no option but to give it. It would not be convincing to object that he was only pretending to give a command in such a case, if he merely went through a duly prescribed procedure in his official capacity. It might be objected instead[11] that we must be careful to distinguish his intentions *qua* official from those he has as a man; and that whilst it is not intelligible that he should indicate that he intends compliance *qua* official whilst, at the same time, saying in his official capacity that he does not intend compliance, it is intelligible that he should indicate that he intends compliance *qua* official but go on to add that as a man he does not. The contrast granted, this is no doubt intelligible. But the point neatly by-passes the central issue, which is whether *qua* official he *has* to intend compliance, or intend to indicate that he so intends; and it is far from clear that he does have to do so.

When various speech acts other than commanding[12] which can be performed by uttering an imperative literally are considered, then the proposed interpretation of *I* becomes even more questionable. 'Try the Cyprus potatoes' says the greengrocer, offering advice, but hardly presuming to intend that you should, since he could, at best, hope or want that you will in view of their price. Jill says 'Knock his helmet off', daring Jack to do so not because she intends that he should, but because she

---

[11] A suggestion made by Anthony Price, whose comments on an earlier draft were most helpful.

[12] In the specific sense in which to command is to require compliance on grounds of one's authority. I owe some of the following examples to Peter Gardner.

is simply curious to see what he will do. And the penitent says 'Forgive me', begging for remission of his penalty, though he cannot intelligibly be supposed to intend that it should be remitted, since it is not within his power to remit it. Such examples could be multiplied; but the general point is that persons performing very many acts belonging to classes (c) and (d) (see p. 74) either can be indifferent to the question whether there is compliance, or else cannot be sensibly supposed to intend it.

(ii) A rather different, and prima facie more interesting, proposal is suggested by some remarks of Alf Ross. He argues that an indicative can be analysed into what he calls a 'topic' and an 'operator' respectively, the function of the latter being to indicate that the 'topic is thought of as real'[13] Thus, 'Peter will shut the door' is analysable as:

(5) (Shutting the door by Peter) so it is.

the bracketed item being the topic. Analogously, it might seem that an imperative can be analysed into a topic and a different operator whose function is to indicate that the topic ought to be, so that 'Peter, shut the door!' is analysable as:

(5) (Shutting the door by Peter) so it ought to be.

To adopt this suggestion would be to 'say that just as the meaning content of (5) is a proposition which may be symbolised as "i(T)" so the meaning content of (6) is a directive properly symbolised "d(T)", where "d" stands for the specific directive element "so it ought to be" '.[14] However, Ross has qualms about the second proposal, for he can neither see what it could mean to say that a topic ought to be real, nor find a common meaning element in this multitude of directives to which the operator 'd' in the formula 'd(T)' refers. Hence, he concludes that 'it must be stressed that the operator "d" ("so it ought to be") does not express a semantic element common to all directives. Its function is to indicate that the action-idea which is the topic is presented as a pattern of behaviour, and is not thought of as real.'[15] Nevertheless, Ross's remarks about the function of 'd' suggest an interpretation which might allow it to express a 'semantic element' common to all imperatives. This is that 'd' has the interpretation 'In the speaker's view there are reasons

[13] Alf Ross (1968), p. 34.
[14] Ibid.
[15] Alf Ross (1968), p. 35.

why the addressee should . . .', its function being to indicate that the speaker believes that there are such reasons. The topic describes the action which, in the speaker's opinion, there is reason for the addressee to perform; and the reasons are understood to be reasons for acting, not just reasons for believing.

Now this proposal is quite plausible given Ross's fundamental thesis that when a directive is uttered the motives which the audience has to conform 'lie not in the utterance itself, but in the circumstances in which the directive is uttered'.[16] So for instance, the reason which an audience may have for heeding the warning 'Look out, snakes!' is that snakes are dangerous; and many other class (c) acts are such that a speaker could obviously believe that a reason why the addressee should do a certain thing is that it is in his interest to do so.

Nevertheless, the account can be seen to be defective when acts from other classes are considered. Perhaps, it can be maintained that commands are such that there is always a reason which the speaker will believe the audience has to conform, namely, the fact that it is required to do so by a legitimate authority. The 'sufficient reason' resides in the will of the commander. But one may have no reason to comply with the demands of someone who insists that one does something, unless threats, inducements, etc. are counted as reasons, for one may have no 'reason' to conform other than fear of the consequences of not doing so. This shows that if the thesis is to be maintained, then 'reason' must be used in a very general sense to include anything which provides a motive for compliance, as well as something which grounds a conclusion of the form 'You should do so and so.' But even when so interpreted, the thesis breaks down completely when confronted with class (d) acts. Often when a person requests something, he is pleased if the audience complies with the request. But it is rather far fetched to suppose that if the speaker knows that his audience has no moral or prudential reason to comply with his request, he nevertheless supposes that a reason which the audience has to comply is that he will be pleased if it does. Certainly, if what is requested is disagreeable and demanding, the fact that the speaker will be pleased if his request is granted is no sort of reason for granting it. Consider too a plea for remission of a

[16] Ibid.

penalty. The speaker will no doubt be very relieved if his request is granted; but if this is the only ground that he has on which to base his plea, and it is surely intelligible that it should be, then he can hardly believe that the competent authority has a reason for granting his plea.[17] Finally, consider a couple of acts from class (c), which are not entirely unproblematical, namely, challenging and daring; does the speaker have to suppose that his audience has a reason for complying when he challenges it, or dares it to do something? May he not challenge his audience to do something quite pointless merely to see how it will react?

The moral is clear: the variety of illocutionary acts which an imperative uttered literally can be used to perform is very great indeed. So too is the variety of intentions, hopes, wishes, etc. with which these acts can be performed, making it extremely unlikely that there is some one of these which is always present, or, at least, is such that the performance of an illocutionary act always counts as a conventional way of indicating its presence.

4. PHRASTICS AND NEUSTICS

Alf Ross's proposal that an indicative is of the form 'i(T)', and an imperative of the form 'd(T)', is a proposal which has been made, in one form or another, very often. There is an obvious attraction in the idea that indicatives and imperatives share a common 'descriptive' constituent, for if this is correct, then the bulk of the work done by the semantical rules for indicatives will not have to be reduplicated for imperatives, since nearly all the rules will apply to what the sentence-types have in common, namely, to topics. There would seem to be a pleasing gain in simplicity, reducing the problem of describing the difference between indicatives and imperatives to that of describing the ways in which 'i' differs from 'd'. Thus, it is of more than passing interest to consider the issues raised by an impressively well-worked-out theory of this sort developed by R. M. Hare.[18]

(i) Hare's theses

Three of Hare's theses are of special interest in the present context:

17 A point which Alan White impressed on me.
18 See, for instance, Hare (1949), and Hare (1952).

(A) That the indicative and the imperative, respectively,

(7) *a* You will shut the door.

     b Shut the door!

are 'both about the same thing, namely, your shutting the door in the immediate future; but . . . they are used to say different things about it'.[19] What the two sentences have in common can be represented by some such phrase as:

Your shutting the door in the immediate future.

which Hare calls a 'phrastic'. Since this tells us only what the sentences are about, it is necessary to add something to distinguish cases in which the speaker says what is the case from ones in which he tells someone to make something the case. This can be done by rewriting (7) *a* and *b* respectively as:

Your shutting the door in the immediate future, yes.

Your shutting the door in the immediate future, please.

the added word in each case being what Hare calls a 'neustic'.

(B) That 'in their ordinary use the common logical connectives 'if', 'and', and 'or', like the sign of negation, are best treated as part of the phrastics of sentences.'[20] Hence, they join phrastics to phrastics, and not sentences to sentences.

(C) That in view of (B) it seems possible 'to reconstruct the ordinary sentential calculus in terms of phrastics only, and then apply it to indicatives and imperatives alike by simply adding the appropriate neustic'.[21] This leads to the so-called 'isomorphism' thesis that to every valid inference with indicative premises and an indicative conclusion, there corresponds a valid inference with imperative premises and an imperative conclusion.[22] Thus, if 'He will go to Birmingham or Leeds' may be validly inferred from 'He will go to Birmingham', then 'Go to Birmingham or Leeds!' may be validly inferred from 'Go to Birmingham!'

I do not propose to discuss the isomorphism thesis in detail. It is, however, worth pointing out that even if it were correct, it would provide only weak confirmation of the correctness of the

---

[19] Hare (1952), p. 18.

[20] Hare (1952), p. 21. Hare does have reservations about saying the same thing about quantifiers, since he is not clear that in ordinary language they behave in the same way in imperatives as they do in indicatives. However, he adds that these differences are purely 'an accident of grammar'.

[21] Hare (1952), p. 26.

[22] See Hare (1949), p. 16.

analysis of indicatives and imperatives into phrastic and neustics, since it is also perfectly compatible with different types of analysis of these sentences. Hofstadter and McKinsey, for instance, argue for a version of the isomorphism thesis, even though they regard 'imperatives as made out of sentences by application of a certain operator.'[23] Thus, for them an imperative is of the form '!S', in which the operator '!' attaches to an indicative sentence, not to a phrastic. Also, it is possible to accept that indicatives and imperatives can be analysed into phrastics and neustics, and yet reject the isomorphism thesis, as is done by Kenny, for instance.[24] There seems to be nothing which is in principle unreasonable in doing this. After all, if neustics have any logical powers at all, it is the isomorphism thesis which is surprising.

Since the isomorphism thesis is logically independent of Hare's analysis, that analysis hardly stands or falls with the thesis. On the other hand, difficulties with (A) and (B) are potentially much more serious, and there are, I want to argue, a number of such difficulties.

(ii) Phrastics

One of the more important questions is whether the supposition that an indicative and its corresponding imperative have a common phrastic really does have the theoretical benefits claimed on grounds of simplicity. These would be very considerable indeed if the analysis applied to interrogatives also; but the supposition that it does immediately runs into problems.

Searle, for instance, has claimed that assertions, requests, and yes–no questions can have a common phrastic—which he calls a 'proposition'. But he points out that which-questions would have to be analysed in a rather different way, and suggests that in their case the interrogative mood indicator attaches to a propositional function, rather than to a proposition.[25] But it is also far from clear that in a yes–no question the interrogative indicator attaches to the sort of item which can occur in both an indicative and an imperative. For not only does a question

23 Hofstadter and McKinsey (1939), p. 447.
24 Kenny (1966).
25 Searle (1969), p. 31.

correspond to each indicative, there is also one corresponding to each imperative. Thus, (8) *b* corresponds to (8) *a*, and (8) *d* to (8) *c*:

(8) *a* I will arrive before midnight.
      b Will I arrive before midnight?
      c Arrive before midnight!
      d Shall I arrive before midnight?

A statement would be an appropriate reply to *b*, a command to *d*. Plainly, if it is supposed that yes–no questions have the same phrastics as indicatives and imperatives do, then both (8) *b* and (8) *d* will be of the form '?*P*', and a quite crucial distinction will remain unmarked. However, if '*P*' is a phrastic, and 'Ind', '!', and '?' stand respectively for the indicative, imperative, and interrogative mood indicators, then one way of marking the difference would be as follows: (8) *a* and *c* are respectively of the form 'Ind (*P*)' and '!(*P*)'; but (8) *b* is of the form '?(Ind (*P*))', whilst (8) *d* is of the form '?(! (*P*))'. Thus, (8) *b* asks a question to which an appropriate response would be a statement whereas (8) *d* asks one to which an appropriate response would be a command, or a piece of advice, etc.[26] Perhaps there are better ways of doing this, but it is difficult to think of one which permits yes–no questions to have a phrastic in common with indicatives and interrogatives.[27]

Of course, the claim that indicatives and imperatives share a common phrastic remains untouched by this. Interestingly however, Searle develops a line of thought which seems to threaten even this claim. After maintaining that there is an important sense in which predication is not a speech act at all, he goes on:

This can be illustrated by considering the following examples, 'You are going to leave', 'Leave!', 'Will you leave?', 'I suggest that you leave'. An utterance of each of these sentences predicates 'leave' of

[26] Boyd and Thorne (1969), p. 57. There is an alternative proposal, namely, that there is a large number of different complex question neustics, '? Ind', '?!', '??', '? promise', '? threaten', etc., which attach to simple phrastics. But this is ruled out on grounds of simplicity, if no other. For we should have to give a separate explanation for each neustic; and would have no single unifying element for '?'. As it is, the basic rule for '?' is clear: that it is a request for a response whose nature is dictated by the sentence to which it is attached.

[27] It must be remembered that not only does each indicative and imperative have its corresponding interrogative, but so does each explicit performative. So, for example, corresponding to 'I, N.N., promise to ø' we have 'Do you, N.N., promise to ø?'

you in a variety of different illocutionary acts. In our canonical notation each is of the form $F\left(\begin{smallmatrix} R & P \\ you & leave \end{smallmatrix}\right)$ where the different values for the variable 'F' mark the different illocutionary forces. But now notice an interesting feature of the relation between the various 'F's' and the 'leave' which does not hold between the 'F's' and the 'you'. The different force indicating devices determine, as it were, the mode in which 'leave' is predicated of you. The F term operates on the predicate term so as to determine the mode in which it relates to the object referred to by the referring term: if the sentence is interrogative, its interrogative character (F term) determines that the force of the utterance is to ask whether the predicate (P term) is true of the object referred to by the subject (R term). If the sentence is imperative, its imperative illocutionary force indicating device (F term) determines that the object referred to by the R term is to do the act specified by the P term, and so on through other examples.[28]

But if the F term affects the 'mode' of predication of the P term what force is left to the claim that in 'Ind (RP)' and '! (RP)' we have the same proposition? For there to be just one proposition, ought there not to be just one univocal mode of predication?

Searle goes on to claim that the F term does not interact with the R term in the way in which it does with the P term:

One might express this difference by saying reference always comes neutrally as to its illocutionary force; predication never comes neutrally but always in one illocutionary mode or another. Even though reference is an abstraction from the total illocutionary act, it is a separate speech act. By analogy, moving the knight is an abstraction from playing chess (because it only counts as moving the knight if you are playing chess), but it is still a separate act. Predication is also an abstraction, but it is not a separate act. It is a slice from the total illocutionary act; just as indicating the illocutionary force is not a separate act, but another slice from the illocutionary act. Why then do we need the notion at all?[29]

Searle's answer is that different illocutionary acts can have the same content, as can be seen from the sentence 'You are going to leave', 'Leave!', and 'Will you leave?' Undoubtedly, 'you' and 'leave' have the same meaning in each of these sentences; but is it necessary to say more than that?

[28] Searle (1969), p. 122.
[29] Searle (1969), p. 123.

It is clear anyway that the theoretical gains of analysing imperatives and indicatives into phrastics and neustics is not anything like as great as it seemed it might be, since it is not an analysis which can be applied to all sentence-types. Indeed, if a phrastic is meant to be a description of a possible state of affairs, then examples involving bound variables, discussed in Chapter 4, Section 4 (iv), below, strongly suggest that it is not even true that all indicatives can be analysed into a phrastic and a neustic. How, for instance, do we disambiguate the pair.

(9) *a* You will catch a fish, but do not eat it!
    b Catch a fish, but don't eat it!

treating 'Your catching the fish, but your not eating it' as the phrastic in each case, as Hare's theory requires, and making use of only one neustic?

The question arises too whether the notion of a phrastic describing a state of affairs, which is employed by Hare,[30] is not logically parasitic on that of a statement being true. In Hare's usage, 'P' describes a situation if and only if 'Ind P' is true, so that the phrastic 'Use of axe or saw by you shortly' describes a state of affairs if and only if it is true that you will shortly use either an axe or a saw.[31] This is hardly surprising, since to describe what is the case is to say that something is true.

At first sight, it does indeed seem that, as Hare maintains, the notion of a content common to an indicative and a corresponding imperative is in principle unproblematical, since a command can always take the form of commanding that the corresponding indicative be made true. But one moral of the examples (9) *a–b* is that the notion of *the* corresponding indicative is suspect; does (9) *a* correspond to 'You will catch a fish, and are not going to eat it', or is it (9) *b* that does? And it is, anyway, unclear that if (7) *a* is analysed as '(Your shutting the door), yes', and (7) *b* as 'Bring it about that "(Your shutting the door), yes" is true', they have a common element 'Your shutting the door', since in (7) *b*, so analysed, it occurs in the opaque context of quotation.

---

[30] Hare (1949), p. 12.

[31] In an interesting paper Stenius distinguishes the truth of a phrastic from that of an indicative; but a phrastic is true if and only if the corresponding indicative is. See Stenius (1969).

(iii) What do connectives connect ?

Hare's claim (B) that 'in their ordinary uses the common logical connectives "if", "and", and "or", like the sign of negation . . . are best treated as part of the phrastics of sentences' is one which, as we saw, he expresses reservations about extending to cover the quantifiers 'all' and 'some'.[32] It seems possible that his claim is also meant to be qualified by the phrase 'in their ordinary uses', though if it is the force of the intended qualification is far from clear. Certainly, Hare must have some reservations about (B), for immediately before advancing the claim that the connectives belong to the phrastic he makes a suggestion which is inconsistent with it, namely that 'the sentence "You may be going to shut the door" might be rendered "I don't say that you are not going to shut the door" or "Your not shutting the door in the immediate future, not–yes!" '[33] Here, of course, the sign of negation qualifies the neustic. Hare is not proposing that 'You may be going to shut the door' is equivalent to 'It is not the case that you are not going to shut the door'!

Another claim which Hare makes which is inconsistent with (B), unless (B) is modified, is that in a hypothetical imperative the 'if-clause itself contains an imperative neustic'.[34] A hypothetical imperative, such as 'If you want to make bread, use yeast', can be distinguished from a conditional imperative, for example, 'If you see anything suspicious, telephone the police', by the fact that *modus ponens* is not valid for it. Thus, treating the major premiss as a hypothetical imperative, the following is invalid:

(10) *a* If you want to make someone mad give him drug X.
     b You want to make Hilda mad.
     c Give Hilda drug X!

The hypothetical imperative tells one only what means to adopt to achieve a given end in a way which does not necessarily endorse the adoption of that end, and hence of the means to it. Thus, someone might say 'If you want to make someone mad give them drug X; but, of course, even if you want to you must

<hr/>

[32] See footnote 20.

[33] Hare (1952), p. 21. This is a view which he repeats elsewhere; cf. Hare (1967), p. 38. He also suggests there that 'I permit you to do not-a' is equivalent to 'not-! a'.

[34] Hare (1952), p. 37.

not try to do so.' On the other hand the following is arguably
valid:

(11) *a* If you want to make someone mad give him drug X.
      b Make Hilda mad!
      c Give Hilda drug X!

The supposition that the antecedent of a hypothetical imperative contains an imperative neustic, as Hare proposes, neatly
explains why (10) is not valid but (11) is, as well as helping to
differentiate a hypothetical imperative from a conditional imperative. For if the antecedent of (10) *a* is imperatival, the mere
fact that you want to make Hilda mad does not license the
inference of the command to give her the drug; but this can be
inferred from (10) *a* together with the command (11) *b* to make
Hilda mad.

Certainly, the example is an instructive one, since it points to
one thing which is highly relevant to the question whether a
subordinate clause which belongs to a sentence *x* itself contains
a neustic, namely, the validity of inferences into which *x*
enters.[35] However, the question of the logical status of hyp-
thetical imperatives is so obscure that it would be unwise to base
much on arguments concerning them. Certainly, it is not
necessary to accept Hare's proposal to account for the apparent
validity of (11). For if (11) *a* is treated, as some have urged it
should be, as an indicative tantamount to 'In order to make
someone mad, you have to give him drug X', then someone who
asserts (11) *a* and commands (11) *b* is in consistency committed
to commanding (11) *c*.

The proposal that (*a*) 'It may be the case that *p*' ('*p*' is a
propositional variable) is equivalent to (b) 'I don't say that
not-*p*', i.e. to (b') 'not-Ind (not-*p*)', should also be rejected for a
number of reasons. It makes the claim made by (*a*) relative to
the speaker in a way in which it surely should not be. Secondly,
if (*a*) is equivalent to (b), then (c) 'Not-(it may be the case that
p)', i.e. 'It is certain that not-*p*', is equivalent to (d) 'I say that
not-*p*'; but we surely cannot infer that it is certain that not-*p*

---

[35] Hare's suggestion is rather tentative. But it might be argued, in the spirit of it,
that (10) is the form '!$P \to$!Q, Ind $P \vdash$!Q', and violates a principle of mood constancy (see D. S. Clarke Jr. (1969)) that a phrastic must remain in the same mood
throughout an argument. On the other hand (11) does not, since it is of the form
'!$P \to$!Q, !$P \vdash$!Q'.

from the fact that I say that not-*p*. Thirdly, and more importantly, in the present context, the proposal has to attribute a more substantial interpretation to 'Ind' than my theory, and the arguments on which it is based, will allow it to bear, in that it has to have something like the force of the performative prefix 'I assert that . . .'. But if the arguments on which the conclusion that the indicative mood indicator can do no more than indicate that the sentence to which it belongs has truth conditions are sound, then a sharp distinction between it and a performative prefix must be made.

However, if performative prefixes can be negated, and it seems clear that they can, [36] then the sign of negation does not always belong to a phrastic, which shows that (B) is not unrestrictedly true. I want now to try to establish further that, even accepting my view of the interpretation of 'Ind' and my tentative view that '!' indicates that the sentence to which it belongs has conformity conditions, logical connectives do not always connect phrastics, but, sometimes anyway, connect sentences (i.e. expressions consisting of both a phrastic and a mood indicator).

(*iv*) *Some counterexamples*

It might seem that the compelling objection to the supposition that a complex sentence can contain more than one neustic (a sentence of mixed mood) is that the status of utterances of such a sentence would be ambiguous to an unacceptable degree. If, for instance, such a sentence contained an occurrence of both the indicative and imperative mood indicators, would a literal and serious utterance of it constitute an attempt to perform the sort of act that can be performed by uttering an indicative, or the sort that can be performed by uttering an imperative?

Certainly, if sentences of mixed mood are to be of any interest, utterances of them must be unambiguously interpretable in a normal speech situation. But is it clear that such sentences could not be? May there not be, for instance, sentences of mixed mood in which one of them is dominant or primary, so that though the presence of the other sentence in the other mood has in some

---

[36] Perhaps the most convincing example is the negation of a command. Thus 'I don't command you to ø' is tantamount to 'I permit you not to ø.'

way to be taken into consideration, it clearly has a subservient role to play? If, for instance, the dominant mood is imperative, and the dominated one indicative, there is no evident reason why it should not be clear that a literal and serious utterance of the sentence as a whole constitutes an attempt to perform the sort of act that can be performed by uttering an imperative—a conditional command would be a case in point. Of course, this does not show that there are sentences of mixed mood, only that there is no objection in principle to such sentences provided that utterances of them are unambiguously construable. It is time to look for such examples, as well as for examples of sentences whose analysis requires more than one mood indicator of the same kind, e.g. two occurrences of '!'.

(a) Interesting examples involving 'and' are, interrogatives apart, difficult to find; here are some:

(12)   *a* He cheeked the policeman, and don't you do it!

      b He worked all night, and who thanked him?

      c Come and sit by me, and why do you ignore me?

As Dummett points out,[37] these examples are not very interesting from a logical point of view, since in each case what is achieved by uttering a complex sentence could have been achieved by uttering two sentences successively. An utterance of (12) *a*, for instance, is tantamount to one of 'He cheeked the policeman' followed by one of 'Don't you do it!'; though it is worth noting that if an utterance of (12) *a* is equivalent to two separate utterances it is necessary for them to be successive. Anyway, logically interesting or not, the examples do show that there can be sentences of mixed mood; moreover, as one would expect, examples involving 'but' can also be found, which in fact turn out to be rather more interesting:

(13)   *a* He is said to be honest, but be on your guard!

      b The coach arrives at midnight, but don't take it!

      c He said he wouldn't do it, but has he?

      d It looks like a Vermeer, but is it?

Now it is not clear that an utterance of (13) *a* would be tantamount to one of 'He is said to be honest' followed by one of 'Be on your guard!', for the implications of the two cases are quite different. In the former the meaning is that you are to be on your guard despite that fact that he is said to be honest—one can

---

[37] Dummett (1973), p. 336.

never be too careful; but in the second the meaning is that the fact that he is said to be honest is a reason for being on your guard. This is so, it seems, because it is natural to take the function of an indicative which is followed by an imperative to be that of stating a reason why the imperative should be complied with. If I say 'It's cold, shut the window!', there is no need to ask why it should be shut. Because this is so utterances of sentences like (13) *a* cannot very naturally be taken to be equivalent to successive utterances of the sentences they contain; for the presence of 'but' signalizes that though there is a reason, statable by use of the contained indicative, not to comply with the imperative, nevertheless one should. Thus, a natural context in which to utter (13) *b* would be one in which you have a good reason to leave on the next coach, but nevertheless I think that you should not do so.

It is obvious that (13) *b* cannot be analysed satisfactorily in such a way that it contains only one phrastic and one neustic. There are two options:

(14) *a* (The coach's arriving at midnight, but your not departing on it), please.

   b (The coach's arriving at midnight, but your not departing on it), yes.

But (14) *a* is not an analysis of (13) *b* but one, at best, of:

(15) Ensure that the coach arrives at midnight and that you don't depart on it!

which is a conjunction of imperatives, meaning that you are to ensure that the coach arrives by midnight, but are not to depart on it. Whilst (14) *b* is an analysis of:

(16) The coach will arrive at midnight, but you will not depart on it.

which is a conjunction of indicatives.

If there are conjunctions of mixed mood, are there also conjunctions whose analysis requires more than one neustic of the same kind? Given my interpretation of 'Ind', it might seem that there is no point in writing (a) 'Ind (P and Q)' as (b) 'Ind P and Ind Q';[38] a conjunction of two items with truth conditions ought to be another item with truth conditions. However, it is nevertheless important to stress the equivalence of (a) and (b). The rule

---

[38] Dummett (1973). It is clear, incidentally, that Dummett's mood indicators have a more substantial interpretation than mine are intended to have.

that from a conjunction one may infer each of its conjuncts does not license one to infer 'Q' from (a) but 'Ind Q', which would be mysterious if (a) were not equivalent to (b). And if an utterance of 'John will come, and Jane will also' is tantamount to one of 'John will come' followed by one of 'Jane will come', as it is, then there is a further reason to stress the equivalence of (a) and (b). For if the complex sentence is a conjunction of *sentences*, then an utterance of it should be tantamount to successive utterances of the sentences it contains. Thus, at least, it is difficult to see that (a) is logically prior to (b), or that it has superior explanatory powers; indeed the boot seems to be on the other foot. Certainly, the fact that (a) has to be treated as equivalent to (b), shows that conjunctions like 'John will come, and Jane will also' can always be treated as conjunctions of sentences.

Given my tentative interpretation of '!', similar remarks apply to the relation between '! (P and Q)' and '! P and ! Q'. And if, as I have assumed, interrogatives are a species of imperative, and if 'Is it raining?' is of the form '?P',[39] then it seems that '?(P and Q)' ought to be equivalent to '?P and ?Q'. Unfortunately, however, it is doubtful whether it is: if I ask (c) 'Did he get there in time and deliver the message?', then the answer 'yes' will mean that each of the questions in (d) 'Did he get there in time? And did he deliver the message?' has 'yes' for an answer. But if the answer to (c) is 'no', then it follows only that at least one of the questions in (d) has 'no' for an answer, but it remains to be determined which. The reason for the non-equivalence of (c) and (d) is twofold; a yes-no question is a question about a specific proposition, so that the object about which a question is raised in (c) is different from the objects in (d). Secondly, yes–no questions ask which of two possibilities obtains: is the proposition in question true, or is it false? This means that there are two possible answers, and which is the correct one is not settled by the question. If a question was simply an instruction to say 'yes', then (c) would be equivalent to (d), since a 'yes' to (c) would be a 'yes' to each of the questions in (d), and vice versa. But since a yes–no question is an instruction to say 'yes' or 'no' depending on what is the case, but does not itself determine what is the correct response, the

---

[39] In the light of earlier remarks a more complicated analysis would probably be appropriate; but the point at issue would be unaffected.

equivalence does not hold; for a 'no' to (c) does not uniquely determine the answers to the questions in (d). So whatever is the correct way to analyse (c), (d) is incontrovertibly a case in which the sign of conjunction has to be taken to conjoin sentences.

There is also no need to conclude, as it seemed that there might be, that it is a mistake to treat interrogatives as a special kind of imperative. What is special about them is precisely the fact that sometimes a correct response is to say 'yes', sometimes it is to say 'no', and that the question itself does not determine which it is. An ordinary request is different, however: the correct response to the request 'Shut the door!' is always to shut the door, and the request itself determines that this is so.[40]

(b) An interesting class of sentences contains the following:

(17) *a* Since he did you a good turn, go and help him!

b I'm tired, so you go!

These cannot plausibly be construed as inferences; and, presumably, Hare would not wish to do so, since so construed they would all violate Poincaré's law. Clearly, in each case the indicative clause can be used to cite a reason why the imperative should be complied with, so that there are two clauses with quite different functions within the same sentence. Hence, a natural way to analyse (17) *b* would be:

(My being tired, yes), so (Your going home, please).

To do so would not be to do anything inconsistent with (B), which is only a thesis about the sentential connectives. But it would undoubtedly complicate the general theory, since it would not always be the case that a complex sentence contains exactly one phrastic and one neustic.[41]

If a phrastic is regarded as descriptive of a possible state of affairs, then the existence of sentences containing bound variables is another likely source of yet further complication.[42]

[40] Strictly speaking we should contrast 'atomic' questions with 'atomic' requests, the point being that the former countenances two possible responses, the latter do not. I do not mean, of course, to deny the existence of disjunctive requests.

[41] Other intresting examples are:

'Tell him that it is raining!'

'Does John know that it is raining?'

'Remind John that it is raining!'

since a plausible case can be made out that each contains an indicative clause.

[42] For an illuminating discssion of this and other difficulties, see Hector-Neri Castañeda (1963).

According to (B):

(9) *a* You will catch a fish, but do not eat it!

should be analysed as '(Your catching a fish, but your not eating it), please'. Part of the problem is that this would have to serve also as an analysis of:

(9) *b* Catch a fish, but don't eat it!

and one might well conclude, as was done in the case of (13) *a–b*, that connectives do not always connect phrastics. But there is in this case an additional reason why it would be difficult to treat an utterance of (9) *a* as tantamount to one of two separate utterances[43] without modifying the notion of a phrastic, since one of the utterances would contain a dangling pronoun.

(*v*) *Conditional commands*

No doubt there are many other prima facie counterexamples to (B), but among them there is one which is of special interest, the conditional command. It is clear why it seems to constitute a counterexample to (B). The antecedent of:

(18) If you walk past the post office, post the letter!

states, it seems, the condition under which the command expressed becomes operative, and so cannot be construed imperatively since an imperative cannot itself state a condition. Hence, the antecedent ought not to be within the scope of the imperative mood indicator '!', and whatever we take to represent the form of (18) we must not take '!(If *A*, then *B*)' to do so. However, if (B) were correct, then (18) would have to be represented in this way, since the neustic must attach to a complex phrastic. Indeed, on certain interpretations of the isomorphism thesis (18) has to be construed as a command (in the generic sense) to make the material conditional 'You will walk past the post office→You will post the letter' true. But that (18) cannot be so construed seems to be shown by the fact that the command to make the material conditional true is conformed with by one who does not walk past the post office, whereas it seems strange at best to say that (18) is conformed with in the same circumstances.

This apparently straightforward argument has been chal-

---

[43] Two utterances could for these purposes count as separate provided that neither contained an expression the meaning or reference of which depended ineliminably on a cross-reference to the other.

lenged by Dummett who maintains that a conditional imperative is to be construed always as a command to make a material
conditional true.[44] We can, he argues, divide conditional imperatives into those whose antecedent is in the power of the
addressee, like (18) and those in which it is not. In the case of
the former there is an overwhelming reason for interpreting the
imperative as a command to make the corresponding material
conditional true, since the addressee may falsify the antecedent in order to comply with the command.[45] Thus, a child
told to wear his coat if he goes out, may choose not to go out in
order to comply with the command. On the other hand, if we
consider a command whose antecedent is not in the power of the
addressee, e.g.:

(19) If anyone tries to escape, shoot him.

then there is no practical difference between the two interpretations. So that though it is possible to interpret such a
conditional as a conditional command it is superfluous to do so.

But what can be meant by saying that it makes no practical
difference which of the two interpretations of (19) is accepted?
Certainly, if no one tries to escape, then it has not been violated;
but might there not be an important practical difference between saying this and saying that it has been complied with?
Suppose that you are a frontier guard and the antecedent of
(19) has remained unfulfilled; then whether we say that you
complied with it, or simply did not violate it, will make a great
deal of difference if you appear before a war crimes tribunal.

The essential question raised by this is whether non-violation
can be equated with compliance; and to this Dummett has an
answer. If we take a paradigm of a speech act which can be
performed conditionally, betting, we find that it has two different outcomes, either the offerer takes the money or the taker
takes the money. A conditional bet is then simply a bet which is
on only if the specified condition obtains; if it does not, then the
bet is off and nobody pays anybody anything. So we can say
that if the condition does not hold, it is as if there had been no
bet. Can sense be made of the idea of a conditional command in

---

[44] Dummett (1958), and (1973), pp. 339 ff. I use 'conditional imperative' for an
imperative which is grammatically conditional; and reserve 'conditional command'
for a command which is conditional on the satisfaction of its antecedent.

[45] Dummett (1973), p. 339.

an analogous way? This would be possible, Dummett argues, if we could identify two independent possible consequences of the giving of a command. A conditional command would then be one which allowed for a case in which neither obtained.

This would be so, for instance, in a society in which the giving of commands was a strictly formalized affair, and obedience to a command brought reward, disobedience to it punishment, perhaps irrespective of the meritoriousness or culpability of the person receiving the command. In that case, it would be perfectly possible to have conditional commands, the convention governing which was that neither reward nor punishment followed when the antecedent was unfulfilled.[46]

But, Dummett continues, in our society things are not as they are in this imagined society. A command specifies what counts as disobedience, and disobedience gives the commander the right to punish or rebuke provided, of course, that he had the right to give it in the first place.

Obedience does not, on the other hand, confer any right to reward or commendation: it is something which a superior authority has a right to *demand*. Thus in our practice punishment/rebuke are differently related to command from reward/commendation. The former are conventionally related, in the sense that the content of the command determines what shall constitute disobedience, and thus what shall be liable to punishment or rebuke (although, of course, a justified plea of actual inability to avoid disobedience serves as a complete excuse); by contrast, no behaviour secures the right to reward or commendation, while they may be given for any voluntary action taken in order to avoid disobeying. The fact that, in the case of a command expressed by a conditional imperative in which the antecedent is not in the agent's power, we should not say that the agent had obeyed just on the ground that the antecedent was false, is thus no ground for construing the imperative as expressing a conditional command: for there is no question of fixing what shall constitute obedience independently of the determination of what shall constitute disobedience.[47]

Hence, non-compliance can be effectively assimilated to obedience, since each ensures immunity to punishment or rebuke, and thus has the same consequence.

[46] Dummett (1973), p. 342.
[47] Dummett (1973), p. 343.

There are two major objections to Dummett's argument. Firstly, he admits that there are possible societies which would employ a conditional command.[48] Indeed, it seems quite likely that such societies exist. A teaching establishment run by some-one imbued with learning theory might well punish disobedi-ence, reward compliance (to reinforce the right response), and do neither in the event that the antecedent of a conditional remained unfulfilled. Secondly Dummett's arguments apply at best only to commands in the specific sense in which a com-mand is an authoritative directive, and to some related class-(b) acts in the classification argued for previously (see p. 74). One indication of the lack of generality of his claim is that whilst it is natural to speak of obedience to a command in the specific sense, it is hardly natural to speak of requests, pieces of advice, or entreaties being obeyed, though one could say that they were complied with. If the more neutral notions of compliance and non-compliance are employed instead of those of obedience and disobedience, then Dummett's point about commands in the specific sense can readily be reformulated. The essential point would be that non-compliance with a command gives the com-mander the right to punish provided that he had the right to give the command, but that compliance has no special con-sequence.

It is doubtful though whether analogous remarks can be made about members of the groups other than (b). Indeed, very different remarks would seem to be appropriate to those in group (d). The basis of their classification as non-hearer inter-ested and non-sanctioned is that the speaker has no right to expect compliance or to reprobate non-compliance. Hence, if his request, entreaty, etc. is complied with he has reason to be grateful to the person who complied, he owes him, one might say, a debt of gratitude. But if it is not complied with he cannot complain, since he had no right to expect compliance, and so non-compliance has no special consequence.

If this is correct, then we reach a different conclusion about conditional imperatives whose antecedent is unfulfilled and which are used to request etc. than Dummett reached about such imperatives used to command. For the speaker owes the addressee no debt of gratitude if he deliberately falsifies the

[48] A point I owe to Anthony Price.

antecedent of such an imperative. This perhaps explains the basis of one's reluctance to accept that (18) is complied with if its antecedent is falsified. For (18) is more likely to be uttered as a request than as a command.

Thus, if a conditional imperative is used to request, the case in which the antecedent is unfulfilled plainly does not assimilate to the one in which the request is complied with, as Dummett argues happens if it is used to give a command. However, the two cases do not *have* to be assimilated, even if the imperative is being used to give a command, since there are possible societies which would differentiate them. Hence, it seems reasonable to distinguish the use of a conditional imperative which is equivalent to a command to make a material conditional true, from its use as a conditional command; and to regard the latter use as a further counterexample to (B).

CHAPTER 6

I. DOING WHAT IS REQUIRED

IF, AS I have argued, imperatives can neither be analysed performatively, as Katz and Postal propose, nor as expressions of
intentions, wishes, etc., then the inescapable conclusion is that
an account of the meaning of an imperative must, like that of an
indicative, relate it (or utterances of it) to possible states of
affairs. But what is this relation?

It will be convenient, at this point, to introduce the term
'directive' to stand for what can be ordered, requested, de-
manded, etc., on the model of 'statement' used to stand for what
can be asserted, denied, conjectured, etc. Thus, a serious and
literal utterance of an imperative on a particular occasion will
constitute a particular directive; and which directive it constitutes will depend on the meaning of the imperative uttered.

Two fairly uncontroversial points now become important.
Firstly, that one can sometimes conform with a directive by
doing any one of a number of different things. Secondly, that,
as has often been pointed out,[1] the direction of 'fit' between a
statement and what will be the case, on the one hand, and a
directive and what will be the case, on the other, is quite different. It is, of course, true that if what is stated is that p and it is
not the case that p, then it is false that p; and it is also true that if
one is directed to do p and it is not the case that p, then the
directive has not been complied with. These remarks are indeed
very similar, yet they conceal an important difference. For
whereas the statement is faulty because false, the directive is not
faulty because it has not been complied with. On the contrary,
what is untoward is a future in which p is not true. Though these
points intersect in various ways, it is worth amplifying them
separately.

(i) The first point is obvious enough. To take a simple example, if someone is told to take a cake from a plate, there are

[1] See Kenny (1966), p. 68.

several things he can do to comply. He can take a meringue, or a
chelsea bun, or a brandy snap, etc. To do any one of these
things is to take a cake; yet what is done in each case may be
different from that done in any other in the sense that there are
directives which can be complied with only by doing it. Or, to
take a different example (which shows, incidentally, that the
point does not depend on the fact that the directive in question
is expressed by a sentence containing the indefinite article), if I
am told to go to London tomorrow, but not told what means of
transport to use, then I can comply by going by car, or by train,
or by plane, etc. And even if the directive explicitly specifies
that I should go by train, then I can comply by going on the
8.35, or the 9.30, etc.

Now, if to understand a given directive one has to know what
one can do to comply with it, and, as the examples just cited
show, there are often several different things one can do to comply, then the question arises whether there is any single unifying
characteristic possessed by these things? The most striking seems
to be that each involves voluntarily producing a minimum
sufficient condition that will bring about the state of affairs
specified by the directive.[2] This is not quite the truism that it
appears to be on first sight, since not any sufficient condition
will do, but only those which are minimal. That this is so is
strikingly supported by the fact that insofar as what someone
does involves doing 'more' than this, he cannot reasonably
claim that the whole of what he does constitutes compliance,
even though part of what he does undoubtedly may do so. For
instance, if when I am told to paint square A red and I paint
circle B red in which A happens to be inscribed, then though I
perhaps did what I was told insofar as I painted A red, I cannot
claim that I did what I was told to when I did what was additionally necessary to paint B red. Or, to take a different case, if
I am asked by Henry to return his copy of *War and Peace*, then
I can comply by wrapping it up and posting it to him. But
suppose I hire a removal firm and have the entire contents of my
flat moved into Henry's flat; undoubtedly Henry gets his book

[2] The importance of giving an account of what is involved in complying with a
directive was made clear to me by Fine (1973). In this paper he inroduces the
notion of a possible fact that exactly verifies a sentence. Thus, though if '*p* & *q*' is
true then '*p*' is, the fact which verifies the former does not verify the latter.

back, but it seems extravagant to contend that I am merely complying with Henry's request. Often, no doubt, excess of zeal is in no way harmful, and it may even be praiseworthy. However, the point is not that it is never possible to justify such excess, but that it cannot be done on the grounds that one is merely doing what one was asked to do.

(ii) The second point, which was that if one is directed to do p but it is not the case that p, then the directive is not at fault, shows that the way in which directives relate to the world is different from that in which statements do. Nevertheless, just as a person cannot understand a statement unless he knows in which possible states of affairs it would be true, and in which false, so a person to whom a directive is addressed cannot understand it unless he knows which possible states of affairs which can be brought about by him are ones in which he would comply with it, and which not. So, for instance, someone could not understand the directive to take a cake unless he knew that a future state of affairs in which he neither took the meringue, nor the chelsea bun, etc. would not be one in which he complied with the directive. One does not understand a statement unless one knows in which possible states of affairs it is true and in which false, and knows that an affirmation of it constitutes a claim that none of the latter obtain. Analogously, someone does not understand a directive unless he knows which possible states of affairs are ones in which he complies with it and which not, and knows that if it is addressed to him he is being enjoined to produce one of the former states of affairs. This points to the important conclusion that a description of the meaning of an imperative will take the form of a description of those states of affairs which, when it has been used to issue a directive, are ones in which the person to whom it is addressed complies with it, and which are not.

Directives thus constitute conditions on future states of affairs; relative to a given directive not all possible future states of affairs are satisfactory, that is, ones in which it is complied with. Satisfactoriness is, therefore, a relative notion, relating a directive and various possible states of affairs. Relative to 'Close the door!', a state of affairs in which one closes the door and leaves the window open is satisfactory, though relative to 'Close the window!' it obviously is not. It should, incidentally, be obvious from the way in which it has been introduced that satisfactoriness is not a moral or an evaluative notion, but simply a relation between a directive and those possible states of affairs in which it is complied with. Whether some or all of those states of affairs ought to exist is an entirely separate question.

My proposal is, therefore, that imperatives can be associated with conformity conditions, just as indicatives can be associated with truth conditions, and that the function of the imperative mood indicator is simply to indicate that the sentence to which it is attached has conformity conditions.

2. TRUTH AND CONFORMITY

Now there is no doubt that an act which can be performed by uttering an imperative is defective if there is no logically possible way of complying with it. The question can always be asked whether a warning, a command, etc. could have been complied with by the person to whom it was addressed. So far so good. Nevertheless, it might be argued that to establish the position which I am arguing for, namely, that imperatives have conformity conditions, the role of '!' being to indicate that this is so, is not to establish that it is possible to identify an imperative without reference to the illocutionary acts it can be used to perform, since it is not possible to say what a conformity condition is without reference to such acts. Pressing the point, it could be urged that viewed abstractly there is nothing to differentiate a conformity condition from a truth condition, since in precisely the same conditions in which a directive is conformed with the corresponding statement is true. Thus, for example, if 'John, shut the door!' is going to be complied with, then 'John will shut the door' is true. To differentiate them we must at least say something about the differences between the illocutionary forces which the literal utterance of sentences with truth conditions can have, and those which the literal utterance of sentences with conformity conditions can have.

If the objection could be sustained, then my position would require rather serious modification, since it would have to be conceded that the difference between two importantly different types of *semantic* condition, truth and conformity conditions, cannot be explained without reference to illocutionary forces. Hence, it would have to be conceded, I think, that certain important aspects of meaning have to be explicated by reference to illocutionary forces; whereas my position is that, indicators of illocutionary force apart, this is not so. However, even if this did have to be conceded, it would still be possible to maintain, as I wish to, that a sharp distinction can be made between the meaning which an indicative or an imperative has, and the illocutionary force of utterances of it. It would be possible to argue, for instance, that once conformity conditions and truth conditions have been differentiated, perhaps by specifying the different sorts of illocutionary act associated with each, there is a clear distinction to be made between a sentence's truth or conformity conditions, on the one hand, and the particular illocutionary acts performed by literal utterances of it, on the other. For the former never uniquely determine the latter.

It would, therefore, not be a total disaster for me to have to concede that truth conditions can be differentiated from conformity conditions only by reference to illocutionary forces. However, I do not see that there is any reason to concede even this. For, even viewed abstractly, there is at least one important difference between the two sorts of condition, since there are truth conditions which have no correlative conformity conditions. The indicative 'John shut the door yesterday', for instance, has truth conditions, but the putative imperative 'John, shut the door yesterday!' either has no conformity conditions, or else has ones which are logically not satisfiable. Doors which are open at present can be shut in five minutes' time; but nothing can now be done to make it true that a door which was open at noon yesterday became closed five minutes later.

Secondly, it is, of course, true that if (a) 'Shut the door!' is going to be complied with, then (b) 'You will shut the door' is true. Hence, the same state of affairs which has to exist for (b) to be true has also to exist for (a) to be conformed with, a fact which may well suggest that from an abstract point of view a conformity condition cannot be distinguished from its corresponding truth condition. However, the state of affairs, your shutting the door, surely cannot itself be said to be a condition of any sort, though it is something which can be mentioned by a condition which relates it to a specific statement or directive.

Moreover, the way in which it is related to a statement is not the same as that in which it is related to a directive. This is shown by the fact that one can formulate a conformity condition as a kind of technical imperative specifying what the person addressed has to do to comply with a given directive, for example: to comply with (a) you have to shut the door. But the truth condition that (b) is true if and only if you shut the door cannot be reformulated as a technical imperative addressed to a prospective audience. On the other hand, it can, perhaps, be reformulated as one addressed to prospective speakers, as follows: do not utter (b) unless the person referred to by 'you' is going to shut the door.[3]

The fact that a conformity condition can be reformulated as a technical imperative seems to be a reflection of the fact that, a non-defective act performed by uttering an imperative is one it is logically possible to comply with. One would also expect that a conformity condition can be reformulated as a technical imperative addressed to an audience and that a truth condition cannot, since a statement is at fault if what is stated to be so is not so, whereas a directive is not if what it directs does not become the case. In conclusion, it seems reasonable to suppose that conformity and truth conditions can be differentiated without reference to specific illocutionary forces by describing the different ways in which they relate possible states of affairs to directives and statements respectively.

3. INTERROGATIVES

I have been assuming that interrogatives are a species of imperative, so that they pose no special problems of principle. This view should be sharply distinguished from another, apparently very similar view, which has often been maintained, that imperatives are a species of request.[4] This view is in fact very different from the one I have been assuming, since a request is an illocutionary act. Hence, if it were correct, at least one sentence-type would have to be analysed performatively; so that,

---

[3] Cf Lewis (1969), p. 185: 'I said that a convention of truthfulness in L constrained the communicator of an indicative, but not the audience; likewise I am now representing the convention (insofar as it applies to imperatives) as constraining the audience of an imperative, but not the communicator.'

[4] For example, see Hare (1949) and Aqvist (1965).

as Katz and Postal have argued, 'Is it raining?' would be equivalent to 'I request that you answer "Yes, it is raining", or "No, it is not raining." '[5]

There is a puzzling fact which suggests that there might be much to be said for a performative analysis of questions, namely, that a given question can, it seems, be used literally to perform only one illocutionary act, that of asking a question. A strong objection to a performative analysis of imperatives is, it will be recalled, that a given imperative can be used literally to perform a wide range of illocutionary acts; but, seemingly, a similar objection cannot be brought against a performative analysis of questions. Thus, consider again our formula IF (2) of Chapter 4:

The meaning of a sentence x so determines the range R of illocutionary forces of utterances of itself that any speaker who utters x literally, and means something by uttering it, will, if he succeeds in performing any act at all, perform one which belongs to R.

But if x is an interrogative, then it seems that R will have only one member, asking a question.

However, reflection suggests that the conclusion has been reached over hastily. For it is plausible to group asking together with inquiring and questioning, as Vendler does.[6] Certainly, 'I ask . . .', 'I inquire . . .', and 'I question . . .' can each be followed by a so-called 'indirect question', as in the following:

(1) *a* I ask you whether there is a remedy.

   b I inquire whether there was a mistaken diagnosis.

   c I question whether he did it.

The first two sound rather strained, but either would be perfectly natural with some such antecedent as 'Since my wife is unwell, . . .'. On the other hand, it might be conceded that while there is plainly a difference between questioning, which implies doubt about what is questioned, and asking, which does not, there is no difference between asking and inquiring.[7] We could, of course, be content with the concession and ignore the qualification; for if questioning and asking are different, then

[5] See Katz and Postal (1964), p. 86.
[6] Vendler (1972), p. 24.
[7] See Bell (1975), p. 205.

an interrogative can be used to perform more than one illocutionary act, which means that the apparent problem that an
interrogative can be used to perform only one illocutionary act
is illusory. But it is worth pointing out that the qualification
seems to be misplaced. To inquire is to seek information one
does not possess, and one way one can do this is by asking a
question. But not every question asked constitutes an inquiry.
When the history teacher asks when the battle of Waterloo was
fought, he is not inquiring about its date. The difference between 'ask' and 'inquire' is, therefore, that the use of the former
carries no implication that the speaker wishes to be informed,
whereas use of the latter does. It is, moreover, not difficult to see
how a direct question can sometimes be used to ask whether p,
and sometimes to inquire whether p. At first sight, it is harder
to see how a direct question could be used to question whether
p. But suppose that someone has just asserted that p, and that S
asks a question Q an answer to which implies that not-p; then
S will readily be seen to be questioning whether p.

We thus have a list of at least three verbs which name acts
that can be performed by literal utterance of an interrogative,
namely:

    (2) 'ask', 'inquire', 'question'

If Webster is to be trusted we can also add 'query', and the
somewhat archaic pair 'quiz' and 'catechize', the latter being
used, for instance, to elicit an answer which has been learned by
rote. There is, therefore, a similar objection to a performative
analysis of questions as there is to one of imperatives, namely,
that an interrogative can be used to perform more than one
illocutionary act. A further objection, which Bell stresses, is that
questions can occur in sentences 'unasked': 'Just as one and the
same proposition may occur in discourse now asserted, now
unasserted, so questions may occur now asked, now unasked.
Logical relations between questions, and between questions and
answers, must hold whether or not the questions are asked.'[8]
The only sort of context in which it seems that a direct question
occurs unasked is exemplified by:

    (3) Is it raining, I wonder.

in which 'I wonder' presumably has a parenthetical occurrence.
Certainly, Katz and Postal's analysis does not seem right here,

---

[8] Bell (1975), p. 198.

viz.: 'The speaker requests you to answer "Yes, it is raining" or "No, it is not raining", I wonder.'[9] For it seems to offer no explanation why (3) is not a question.

Examples like (3) apart, the case for the thesis that questions can occur unasked presumably rests on the existence of indirect questions. Baker, for instance, has argued that

there is a type of complement in English, occurring with verbs such as *ask, know, decide, matter,* and *depend,* which deserves to be referred to by the name 'question', and that this construction is different from the relative clause construction, despite the superficial similarity between them.[10]

If he is right, then the complements of each of the following contains a nominalized question:

(4) *a* John knows why she did it.
    b John told me who killed Smith.
    c John found out when Mary left.

There do seem to be very good grounds adduced by Baker for distinguishing the subordinate clauses in these sentences from relative clauses, though this in itself is insufficient to establish that they are questions. An argument of Austin's (which Baker also employs) is, therefore, interesting since it suggests how a question is involved in (4) *a–d*:

In this respect, 'I can smell what he is smelling' differs from 'I can know what he is smelling'. 'I know what he is feeling' is not 'There is an *x* which both I know and he is feeling', but 'I know the answer to the question "What is he feeling?" ' And similarly with 'I know what I am feeling': this does *not* mean that there is something which I am *both knowing and feeling.*[11]

Certainly, an account of the meaning of, for example, (4) *a* should have the consequence that it is true if and only if John can answer the question 'Why did she do it?'; and similar conditions obviously apply to (4) *b* and *c*. Thus, a question can be said to occur in such sentences in the sense that an account of

[9] That this would be their analysis is clear from Katz and Postal (1964), p. 110. If, as Anthony Price suggested to me, 'wonder' is parsed as 'ask oneself', then the oddity is somewhat diminished; though the performative reading of Q (the question morpheme) blocks the natural reading of (3), viz. 'I ask myself whether to say "Yes, it is raining" or "No, it is not raining." '
[10] Baker (1970), p. 124.
[11] Austin (1961), p. 64.

their meaning has to mention a specific question. On the other hand, the fact that the question is *mentioned* makes it natural to put it in quotes, as Austin does in his suggested paraphrase; and it could, of course, be argued that this is precisely why it does not have the force of a question when it occurs in sentences like (4) *a–c*. Certainly, there seems to be no reason why Katz and Postal should not agree that questions do occur unasked in the cases in question, but go on to add that this is not an argument against their analysis since they occur in 'quotes' which deprive them of their customary force. At first sight, Baker's criticism that Katz and Postal's arguments for positing a question morpheme *Q* fall apart when confronted with indirect questions seems conclusive. For, as Baker points out, the syntactic arguments apply to indirect questions as well as to direct ones, since the same co-occurrence restrictions apply in both cases. Yet the semantic argument that we need to be able to explain why 'Is it raining?' has the force of a request hardly applies to indirect questions. But if in sentences like (4) *a–d* questions occur only in quotes, then the facts which Baker draws attention to are hardly surprising.

In conclusion, there is undoubtedly a case for maintaining that questions can occur unasked, particularly in view of (3), and the fact that this is so raises a number of fundamental difficulties for a performative analysis of questions. However, it seems that arguments against the performative analysis based on considerations about indirect questions are somewhat inconclusive.

4. WHAT IS SPECIAL ABOUT INTERROGATIVES?

(i) If interrogatives are a species of imperative, what is distinctive about them? It is customary to distinguish 'yes–no' questions such as:

(5) Is it raining?

from wh-questions, such as:

(6) Which one shall I take?

One characteristic of both types of question is that appropriate responses to them involve either performing, or refraining from performing, illocutionary acts. Thus, a statement is a possible reply to (5), though not all yes–no questions have statements as replies. The answer 'Take it' in reply to the question 'Shall I

take it?' will be a command, or a piece of advice, etc.; whilst
the answer 'I promise' to the question 'Do you promise to go?'
is, of course, a promise. Note though that whilst both the possible answers to (5), namely, 'It is raining' and 'It is not raining',
are statements, we do not have as possible answers to 'Do you
promise to go?' the pair of promises 'I promise to go' and 'I
promise not to go.' Only the first of these is an answer to the
question, the other possible answer being 'I do not promise to
go', to utter which is not to promise not to go, but to refrain
from promising to go.

Now it is natural to suppose that yes–no questions determine
at least partially, the type of reply expected; for if they did not,
how would one know what sort of reply was appropriate? This
they do, it seems, by confronting the person questioned with a set
of sentences, his task being, in the simplest case, to utter literally
and seriously at least one of them. Hence, the type of sentence
belonging to the disjunction will determine, at least partially,
the type of act to be performed. For instance, if the sentences
are all imperatives, then the type of act to be performed will, at
least, have to be the sort that can be performed by a literal and
serious utterance of an imperative. Hence, the second member
of each of the following pairs is a plausible, if incomplete,
analysis of the preceding sentence:

(7) *a* { Is it raining?
Affirm one of the following: It is raining, It is not
raining.

b { Shall I go?
Affirm one of the following: Go!, Do not go!

c { Do you promise to go?
Affirm one of the following: I promise to go, I do not
promise to go.

Moreover, it is obviously possible to specify, in the way in
which we did for imperatives, what the person to whom a given
question is addressed can do to comply with it. For example, to
comply with (7) *a* one performs the sort of act that can be performed by a literal and serious utterance of one of the presented
sentences; the understanding being, perhaps, that if one is not
in a position to sincerely utter either, one says so.

Thus, the claim that yes–no questions are a species of imperative is defensible in depth. Each one can be complied with by

performing, or refraining from performing, an illocutionary act whose nature is partially determined by the question itself. At first sight, this does not adequately distinguish them from other imperatives, since one can command, request, beg, etc., the performance of an illocutionary act. However, if (7) *c* is contrasted with:

(8) Promise to go!

a difference which we have already commented on emerges. Every possible way of complying with (8) constitutes a case of promising to go, whereas (7) *c* can be complied with either by sincerely promising, or by refraining from promising. What is special about (7) *c*, therefore, is that sometimes it has the answer 'I promise', and sometimes it does not, and that the question itself does not determine which is the correct one in a given case.

The analysis of wh-questions is much more complicated. But it seems reasonable to maintain that the appropriate response always involves performing an illocutionary act. This marks one difference from yes–no questions, since refraining from performing an illocutionary act is never an appropriate response in this case. The question 'Which one do you promise to buy me' has 'I promise to buy you the red one', for example, as a possible answer; but 'I do not promise to buy you one' seems not to be an answer to the question but a correction of its presupposition that I have promised to buy you one. If you do wish to find out directly whether I am prepared or not to buy you one of them, you should have asked the yes–no question 'Do you promise to buy me one?' A further difference is that wh-questions contain an open sentence and implicitly present a set of sentences by means of it, each member of which is a substitution instance of the open sentence. Thus, if the question is 'Who did you see?' the relevant set is obtained by making appropriate substitutions in 'I saw x.' The elaboration of this account encounters many difficult problems, and it seems possible that such questions as 'How did he do it?' and 'Why did he do it?' require special treatment.[12] However, the complexities do not seem to threaten the thesis that interrogatives are a species of imperative.

Incidentally, it is clear on this account why '$?(p \& q)$' differs from '$?p \& ?q$'. The former has as possible answers '$p \& q$' and

[12] See Bromberger (1966), p. 604.

'-(p&q)'. But the second of these answers does not tell one whether to answer '?p&?q' with 'yes' to the first question and 'no' to the second, or with 'no' to the first and 'yes' to the second, or with 'no' to both of them.

(ii) Since my account does not give a performative analysis of interrogatives, it does not unduly limit the range of acts which an interrogative can be used to perform as does the account given by Katz and Postal. On the other hand, it seems that my account also runs into serious trouble when confronted with such sentences as:

(3) Is it raining, I wonder.

If we expand this on the lines of the partial analysis proposed we get something which seems to be no improvement on the proposal criticized earlier, namely:

(3') Affirm one of the following: It is raining, It is not raining, I wonder.

However, if 'wonder' is parsed as 'ask oneself', and it is assumed that a question can be nominalized when it occurs as the filling for a container verb, the result seems quite natural:

(3") I ask myself whether to affirm one of the following: It is raining, or it is not raining.

The meaning of (3") is that the speaker is curious about the answer to that question which one responds to, provided one can do so sincerely, either by affirming that it is raining, or that it is not.

5. THE ISOMORPHISM THESIS

If the claim that directives are related to possible states of affairs in a way which is different from that in which statements are is correct, then, if directives have a logic,[13] it would be surprising if it were strictly isomorphic to that of statements. The different relations involved ought, on the face of it, to make some difference. Reverting for a moment to the terminology of 'phrastics' and 'neustics', the point could be put by noting that if the isomorphism thesis were correct, then if 'Ind' is replaced

---

[13] For the case against, see, for instance, Williams (1963) and Sellars (1963); and for the case for, see Geach (1963). There is, of course, no question that directives can be inconsistent with each other. What is more questionable, and it is to this point that sceptics about imperative logic attach importance, is whether if each one of a set of imperatives is used with, for example, the force of a command, one can infer a further imperative with that force from them.

throughout by '!' in a valid pure indicative inference (i.e. one in which all the premisses and the conclusion are indicatives), the result will always be valid, and vice versa. But if 'Ind' and '!' have any logical powers at all, the conclusion is an unexpected one, for if they have, the presence of one rather than another ought to make a difference sometimes.

Hare, of course, acknowledges that which combination of neustics is involved is a crucially important question with mixed inferences, i.e. ones involving both indicatives and imperatives, in formulating the principle:

> No indicative conclusion can be validly drawn from a set of premisses which cannot be validly drawn from the indicatives amongst them alone.[14]

However, acceptance of this principle leaves him with an extremely puzzling question to explain: Why if antilogism is valid for pure indicative inferences and hence, on his account, for pure imperative ones as well, is it not valid for mixed inferences? For given his principle, he must say that even if the following:

(9) If you stand by Jane, do not look at her!
    You are standing by Jane.
    Do not look at her!

is valid, which it surely is, the following inference, which can be obtained by antilogism from (9), is not valid:

(9') If you stand by Jane, do not look at her!
     Look at her!
     You are not standing by her.

Certainly, it seems to be no more reasonable to deny Hare's principle and maintain that antilogism is valid for mixed inferences than it is to hold on to his principle and deny that antilogism is valid in the case in question. So without further discussion of Hare's principle, the example can hardly be taken to show that mood indicators can affect the validity of mixed inferences, though a question perhaps remains why an analogous principle is not true of imperatives. No one would claim that an imperative conclusion can be validly drawn only from the premisses of an argument which are themselves imperatives. However, since there are, unquestionably, mixed inferences whose validity does depend on which combination of neustics is

[14] Hare (1949), p. 28.

present, there is no need here to pursue the question of the truth of the principle further. Consider, for example, the inference:

(10) Varnish every piece of furniture you make!
   You are going to make a table.
   Varnish it!

which is prima facie valid, though the result, (10′) below, of switching the order of the neustics in the premisses is certainly not:

(10′) You are going to varnish every piece of furniture that you make.
   Make a table!
   Varnish it!

Clearly, examples like these, together with ones which Poincaré's law is designed to deal with,[15] show that neustics do have properties which can affect the validity of inferences into which they enter, and it is this which makes it difficult to see how the isomorphism thesis can be true. Hence, a brief examination of a criticism of the thesis in a particular case would seem to be well worth while.

6. A DISPUTED INFERENCE

It seems that Alf Ross was the first to argue that the isomorphism thesis is mistaken, on the grounds that the inference:

(11) Post the letter!
   Post the letter or burn it!

is not valid.[16] The case for rejecting (11) has been ably stated by Bernard Williams,[17] who argues that its premiss and conclusion have what he calls 'permissive presuppositions' which are inconsistent with each other. Given the premiss, the natural assumption is that the addressee is not permitted not to post the letter; but given the conclusion one assumes that he is permitted to post it and permitted to burn it.[18] Thus, the conclusion gives the addressee a choice which he did not have before,

---

[15] Poincaré's law is, of course, the principle that a valid inference cannot have an imperative conclusion unless it has at least one imperative premiss.

[16] Alf Ross (1944), p. 38.

[17] See Williams (1963).

[18] I perhaps state the argument at this point more strongly than Williams would wish to, because I believe that to permit someone to do p or q is to permit him to do p and to permit him to do q (see Kamp (1973)). A more modest claim, which is sufficient for Williams's argument, is that the permissive presuppositions of the conclusion include permission to burn the letter provided that one does not post it, and permission not to post it provided one burns it.

so that the utterance of it would have a 'cancelling effect, the effect of withdrawing what has already been said', which effectively prevents us construing (11) as an inference.[19]

In an interesting reply,[20] Hare points out that the crucial question raised by this argument concerns the status of the permissive presuppositions; are they entailments, or is some weaker relationship involved? He goes on to argue that whilst the premiss's permissive presupposition is entailed by it,[21] the conclusion's is only a conversational implicature. Hence, there is no formal inconsistency, though there would be if the conclusion entailed its permissive presuppositions. For, in that case, the premiss would entail 'You are not permitted not to post the letter', whilst the conclusion would entail, amongst other things, 'You are permitted not to post the letter (i.e. to burn it).' Hare argues also that imperative inferences are not the only inferences which can have premisses which entail things which are inconsistent with things conversationally implicated by their conclusions, since indicative inferences can also.

An example of an indicative inference which is of this kind is, according to Hare, involved in the following case:

If, being absent-minded, I ask my wife 'What have I done with the letter?' and she replies that I have posted it or burnt it, she conversationally implicates that she is not in a position to say which I have done; . . . She also conversationally implicates that I may not have posted it, so long as I have burnt it.[22]

Similarly, he maintains, the future tense indicative:

(12) You are going to post the letter or burn it.

has the conversational implicature:

(13) You may be not going to post the letter, so long as you are going to burn it.

However, he concludes, it might be thought that (13) is

in some sense inconsistent with the statement 'You are going to post the letter'. But we do not commonly hear it argued that the inference from 'p' to 'p or q' in the indicative mood is inadmissible because 'p' is inconsistent with a conversational implicature of 'p or q'.[23]

[19] Williams (1963), p. 33.
[20] Hare (1967).
[21] Hare (1967), p. 27.
[22] Hare (1967), p. 28.
[23] Hare (1967), p. 29.

But assuming that (13) is equivalent to:

(13') So long as you are going to burn the letter, it may be that you are not going to post it.

it is difficult to see in what way it is inconsistent either with:

(14) You will post the letter.

or with anything which is entailed by it; yet if the analogy which Hare is trying to establish holds, there must be such an inconsistency. Certainly, if it is possible for (14) to be true, and for it to be false that you are going to burn the letter, as it surely is, then (14) and (13) must be consistent. Hence, the possibility of saying without becoming inconsistent that Eclipse will win, but that, of course, he may not if it rains. For someone who says this can go on to say that it is quite certain that it will not rain.

A further point which Hare makes seems, at first, to be more convincing. If, he argues, having inferred 'Do p or q!' from 'Do p!' one does p, then one has indeed erred. 'But his error consists not in making an invalid inference, but in fulfilling the weaker command when what I gave him was the stronger. We cannot in general be sure of fulfilling commands by fulfilling other commands which are inferable from them.'[24] So, for example, someone who only jumps out of an aeroplane does not fulfil the command 'Put on your parachute and jump out!'; he has done only what is necessary, but not sufficient, to fulfil it. But commands do not differ from statements in this respect, 'except that fulfilment takes the place of belief (which is the form of acceptance appropriate to statements)'.[25] Hence, someone who is told 'Smith put on his parachute and jumped out' is entitled to believe that Smith jumped out; but if he believes that this is all that Smith did he is in error.

However, as Edgley points out in an excellent discussion,[26] the relation which belief has to statements is, in a number of important respects, quite different from that which fulfilment has to directives. For if $\{p,q\}$ is inconsistent, it is nevertheless logically possible that someone should believe that p and believe that q; but it is not logically possible for someone to fulfil (i.e. comply with) both of the corresponding directives '!p' and '!q'.

[24] Ibid.

[25] Hare (1967), p. 30. The view that fulfilment (compliance) is the form of acceptance appropriate to commands whilst belief is the form appropriate to statements is developed at greater length in Hare (1952), p. 20.

[26] Edgley (1969), p. 170.

Thus, whilst compliance with '$!p$' is a necessary condition of compliance with '$!(p\&q)$', a belief that p is not a necessary condition of a belief that $p\&q$; for, however unlikely it is, it is logically possible for someone to have the latter belief without having the former.

Indeed, even if the relation which belief has to statements is the same as that which fulfilment has to directives, Hare's argument fails.[27] It is true that someone who complies with 'Post the letter or burn it!' may do something inconsistent with 'Post the letter!' from which it is, according to Hare, inferable. So, if one is at liberty to comply with a directive which one has inferred from a set of directives each one of which has been addressed to one—and if one is not, then there does not seem to be much point in talking about imperative inference—then compliance with '$!(p$ or $q)$' may preclude compliance with '$!p$'. But if someone only believes that Smith jumped out of the aeroplane, then what he believes (that he jumped out of the plane) is indeed inferable from what he believes when he believes that Smith put on his parachute and jumped out of the plane, but it is also consistent with it. If, on the other hand, he believes that the-only-thing-Smith-did was to jump out of the aeroplane, then though what he believes is not compatible with what he believes when he believes that Smith put on his parachute and jumped out, it is not inferable from it either.

One interesting question which remains is whether

(15) You may burn the letter provided you don't post it.

is, as Hare claims, merely a conversational implicature of an utterance of:

(16) Post the letter or burn it!

The only argument that I can find which Hare gives in support of this contention is that the implication is cancellable, that is, that an utterance of (16) can be followed consistently by one of the negation of (15). He claims, in illustration of his point, that an army Transport Officer who has decided that the trucks under his command shall travel to Scotland either via Coldstream or via Berwick might 'say to the commander of the convoy "Go via Coldstream or Berwick: I'm not saying which at the moment, and I'm not authorizing you yet to take the Coldstream route; report to the Transport Officer at Newcastle

[27] See Edgley (1969), p. 173.

and he will give you a further message from me." '[28] This, Hare maintains, shows that 'You may go via Coldstream if you don't go via Berwick' is only a conversational implicature of an utterance of 'Go via Coldstream or Berwick!', since one can consistently follow an utterance of the latter by a withdrawal of permission to go via Coldstream if the route via Berwick is not taken, without having to withdraw the command to go via Coldstream or Berwick itself.

However, it seems to me that the Transport Officer's way of expressing himself is extremely eccentric. What he should say, surely, is 'Prepare to go either via Coldstream or Berwick'; this instruction is perfectly clear, and plainly does not give permission to go via either Coldstream or Berwick. There would, therefore, seem to be no need to utter 'Go via Coldstream or Berwick!' and follow it with such a complicated series of qualifications. Indeed, to say 'Go either via Coldstream or Berwick, but you may not go via Coldstream if you do not go via Berwick and you may not go via Berwick if you do not go via Coldstream' is reminiscent of Henry Ford's joke that people can choose what colour car they like, provided it is black, in that the qualifications empty the command of all content.

How then is (15) related to an utterance of (16) if it is not a conversational implicature? It is difficult to avoid the conclusion that to utter (16) to give a command *is*, amongst other things, to give the permission expressed by (15). For, presumably, an utterance of (16) to give a command cannot be followed consistently by one of:

(17) You are not permitted to post the letter or burn it.

since one cannot consistently follow a command to do p by a prohibition against doing it. Hence, an utterance of (16) to give a command is to give the permission:

(18) You are permitted to post the letter or to burn it.

The crucial question, therefore, is 'What is involved in giving this permission?'

Han Kamp has argued cogently that to give permission to do something is in effect to lift a prohibition against doing it.[29] Thus, to permit one's daughter to stay out after 11 p.m. is to lift the prohibition against doing so. Does 'You are permitted

[28] Hare (1967), p. 32.
[29] See Kamp (1973).

to do *p* or *q*' lift a wider set of prohibitions than 'You are permitted to do *p*' does? Kamp maintains that it does, and that this is what one would expect given the meaning of 'or': 'For as logicians have realized with regard to assertions for at least a century "or" stands for set theoretic union. The set of situations in which a disjunctive assertion is true is the union of the sets of possible situations which realize its disjuncts.'[30] Certainly, 'You are permitted to do *p* or *q*' cannot be just a permission to do *p* or *q* without one to do *p* provided that one does not do *q*, or one to do *q* provided that one does not do *p*, for that would be an empty permission. Nor is it just a permission to do *p*, nor just one to do *q*, for if it was either of these things there would never be any point in uttering 'You are permitted to do *p* or *q*' rather than 'You are permitted to do *p*' or 'You are permitted to do *q*'. The inescapable conclusion seems to be that to give permission to do *p* or *q* is to give permission to do *p* provided one does not do *q* and permission to do *q* provided one does not do *p*. Hence, there is no question of uttering (16) to give a command and, at the same time, refusing to grant the permission (15). Further, in view of the principle that to command *p* is to prohibit not-*p*, there can be no question of consistently following an utterance of:

(19) Post the letter!

with a withdrawal of the prohibition:

(20) You are forbidden not to post it.

unless, of course, one is prepared to withdraw (19). Hence, the premiss and conclusion of (11) have (15) and (20) respectively associated with them in a very intimate way indeed; yet (15) and (20) are, on the face of it, inconsistent.

[30] Kamp (1973), p. 67.

CHAPTER 7

In this chapter I want to discuss a number of issues involved in the extension of my proposals to other sentence-types, and also some connected with the formula IF (2) (see p. 52).

I. SUBJUNCTIVES AND TRUTH CONDITIONS

(i) The subjunctive is often counted as a distinct mood, though some linguists deny that English has a proper subjunctive.[1] The controversy whether it has is one which I am not competent to enter into, and I shall content myself here with simply citing a number of examples which involve the subjunctive if any English sentences do, viz.:

(1)   *a* If I were there, there would be no trouble.
     b I wish that I were there.
     c Would that I were there.
     d It is time that you were there.
     e It is necessary that everyone read the instructions.
     f We demand that he be reinstated.

Each of these sentences carries at least a strong implication that the state of affairs referred to by the subjunctive clause either does not, or may not obtain. For example, each of (1) *a–c* implies the falsity of:

(2) I am there.

One cannot, of course, make this into a definition of a subjunctive, since the use of a past tense rather than a present one can have exactly the same effect, as in:

(3) If I was there, there would be no trouble.

This, is, presumably, one of the things which makes isolation of the subjunctive difficult.

The main problem posed for my account by the subjunctive is that a subjunctive conditional (for example, (1) *a*) can have

---

[1] See, for instance, Palmer (1965), p. 48: 'the notion of a subjunctive mood is a simple transfer from Latin and has no place in English grammar, since all the potential subjunctives turn out to be past tense in form (or to be the simple uninflected form as in "God save the Queen").'

truth conditions,[2] yet I have identified the indicative mood with the possession of truth conditions. At first sight, it might seem that subjunctive clauses can only occur in subordinate clauses, and that this provides the basis for a solution. But certain formulaic utterances, e.g. 'God save the Queen!', present awkward counterexamples. And though the fact that the use of an unembedded indicative which expresses a proposition p neither implies not-p, nor it may be the case that not-p, is striking, it is difficult to see how appeal can be made to this fact when formulating a criterion, if most subjunctive conditionals never occur unembedded. Perhaps the best solution is to combine the two ideas, and say that an indicative can occur unembedded, and that if p is the proposition it expresses, the use of it when it so occurs neither implies not-p, nor it may be the case that not-p.

Interestingly, it would not seem possible to associate the subjunctive mood with a particular illocutionary act. It might be suggested that (1) a has:

(1) a' Suppose that I were there, then there wouldn't be any trouble.

as a rough paraphrase. But even if it can, (1) e and f, for instance, surely cannot be paraphrased in a way which involves 'suppose'; and the fact that (1) a could be paraphrased in this sort of way would not mean that it could be associated with any particular illocutionary act, such as postulating. Clearly, (1) a' has to be sharply distinguished from:

(1) a'' I postulate that if I were there, then there would not be any trouble.

In fact, the 'rough' paraphrase (1) a' is very rough indeed, since (1) a can be prefixed by a wide range of performative prefixes which (1) a' cannot, including 'I admit that . . .', 'I maintain that . . .', and 'I conjecture that . . .'. The fact that it can shows that (1) a, uttered literally, can be used to perform many of the acts which sentences with truth conditions can. This is, of course, as it ought to be, if (1) a has truth conditions, and the possession of truth conditions is a determinant of illocutionary force. However, as (1) c and (1) f show, not all sentences with subjunctive clauses have truth conditions; and if there were any doubt about this, it would be dispelled by consideration of such

[2] For a contrary view see Mackie (1962).

'hypothetical' questions as 'If you were in a position to do it, would you?' Indeed, as these examples make plain, the range of illocutionary acts which can be performed by literally uttering sentences which contain subjunctive clauses is very wide indeed. But the fact that this is so is hardly surprising if a subjunctive clause is nearly always a subordinate clause.

(ii) The existence of the subjunctive as a separate category is, as was pointed out, disputable; but our discussion of the subjunctive conditional, which was prompted by the observation that it has truth conditions, raises the interesting question whether it might not be possible to make finer distinctions within the category of sentences which have truth conditions than I have done, and then associate with each sub-category a distinctive sub-set of illocutionary acts. This is not a possibility which I shall examine in detail; but the formal semantics of modal logic suggest that sentences of the form 'It is logically necessary that p' and 'It is logically possible that p' can be differentiated by the fact that their truth conditions are concerned not only with what is true in this world, but with what is true in other possible worlds. Whether the semantics of formal modal systems greatly illuminate the notions of necessity and possibility employed by natural languages is plainly a matter of legitimate philosophical dispute. But insofar as it is reasonable to suppose that there is something distinctive about the truth conditions of modal sentences, then it is plausible to suppose that there is a principled way of isolating a distinct category of modal sentences. It could well be that it is possible to distinguish other sub-categories of sentences which have truth conditions in a similar sort of way, and that each such sub-category determines slightly different ranges of illocutionary acts.

One way then in which one could try to enrich my account would be by trying to make finer distinctions within the categories of sentence-types already distinguished. Another way would be by trying to extend the account to cover further sentence-types.

2. COMMISSIVES

An interesting group of acts which Vendler groups together under the title of 'commissives' includes promising, undertaking, pledging, and swearing; but is it possible to associate a type of

sentence with this group of acts which can, in suitable circumstances, be used literally to perform each one of them?

Consider, to begin with, the report:

(4) Smith said that he would be there.

This might be a report of a mere statement of intention, or of a
promise, or an undertaking, etc., and the fact that this is so
suggests that the present tense of the sentence embedded in (4),
or the variant obtained by replacing 'will' with 'shall', viz.:

(5) I will/shall be there.

is a sentence which Smith could have used, in appropriate circumstances, to perform each one of these acts. Interestingly, (5)
neatly embeds in the frames:

$$I \left(\begin{array}{l} \text{promise} \\ \text{undertake} \\ \text{pledge} \\ \text{swear} \\ \ldots\ldots \end{array} \right) \text{ (to) you that } \ldots\ldots\ldots$$

as one would expect.

The sentence (5) can, of course, have the use of an indicative,
which raises the question of the legitimacy of distinguishing a
distinct commissive use. Interestingly, therefore, there can be
grammatical indications that (5) is an indicative rather than a
commissive. If it is prefixed by certain sentence adverbs, for
example, 'probably' and 'possibly', then it is unambiguously an
indicative, whilst if it is followed by 'without fail' it is unambiguously a commissive. Secondly, as Palmer points out,[3] 'Mary
will not be met by me at the station' is not the passive of the
commissive 'I will not meet Mary at the station'; though it is the
passive of the indicative 'It will not be the case that I meet
Mary at the station.'

It is necessary also to distinguish the question 'Are you going
to the dance?' from the apparently similar 'Will you go to the
dance?' The former has 'I am going to the dance' and 'I am not
going to the dance' as possible answers, the utterance of either
of which constitutes a report, or a statement, etc. It would be
appropriate to put this question, for instance, to someone whose
programme of activities is being arranged for him; so that if he
has not yet found out what that programme is, he can point out

[3] Palmer (1965), p. 108.

that he is not in a position to answer, because he has not discovered yet what he is going to do. The second question, on the other hand, has as possible answers 'I will go to the dance' and 'I won't go to the dance.' An utterance of the first will constitute a statement of intention, or an undertaking, etc., whilst one of the second will be a statement of intention, or a refusal. It is clear that this question, unlike the first, is one it will be appropriate to put not to someone whose programme is being arranged for him, but to someone who has to decide for himself whether to go to the dance.

A statement expressed by the indicative (5) is, of course, true if and only if the speaker goes to the place he refers to by use of 'there'. A possible state of affairs which has to exist for a statement expressed by (5) to be true is clearly also intimately related to its use as a commissive, since the commissive (5) is complied with if and only if the speaker goes to the place he refers to by the use of 'there'. However, as is the case with imperatives, the relation between the possible state of affairs and the commissive is not the same as that between it and the corresponding indicative. The difference is, in this case, that it is up to the speaker to conform by performing the action which is referred to, rather than the person to whom the sentence is addressed.[4] If I utter 'You will be there!', it is up to you to conform by going there, but if I utter 'I will be there' as a commissive, then it is up to me to conform by going there. This is an important difference; but in spite of it, it seems that many of the points made about conformity in the former case apply also in the second. For instance, it seems clear that compliance in both cases involves producing a minimum sufficient condition, not just doing anything which involves incidentally producing the specified state of affairs. Finally, given that the speaker acts in conformity with (5) by going to the place which he refers to by use of 'there', there seems to be no problem in principle in seeing how the sentence can be used literally, in appropriate circumstances, to perform such acts as undertaking, or promising, to go there.

---

[4] See Lewis (1969), p. 187: 'In the case of the indicative "I shall return", to be truthful is to try *before* I utter the sentence to make my words correspond to my deeds. . . . In the case of the commissive "I will return", to be truthful is to try *after* I utter the sentence to make my words correspond to my deeds.'

3. SERIOUSNESS AND LITERALNESS

(i) Comment is called for on various issues raised by IF (2) which, for convenience, I repeat:

The meaning of a sentence x so determines the range R of illocutionary forces of utterances of itself that any speaker S who utters x literally, and means something by uttering it, will, if he succeeds in performing any act at all, perform one which belongs to R.

To begin with, it might be suggested that the clause 'and means something by uttering it' could be replaced simply with 'seriously'. A serious utterance is sometimes said to be one which is not a joke, not in a poem, not in a play, etc.; but the force of the 'etc.' is far from clear, so that a more explicit explanation is desirable. On the other hand, one cannot, for present purposes, simply characterize a serious utterance as one which has a serious purpose. The joking 'If you fell down, you'd never get up' is, no doubt, not an assertion; but by uttering it the speaker may certainly intend to convey in a roundabout way that you are eating too much, and thus have a serious purpose. It might, perhaps, be suggested that an utterance is serious only if an illocutionary act is attempted; but that would make the condition that an utterance has to be serious to determine a range of illocutionary acts unilluminating. The advantage of the clause 'and means something by uttering it', is, therefore, that it is explicit and, secondly, that it is one which it is reasonable to think can be explicated in a non-trivial way using the insights of Grice (1969) and Schiffer (1972).[5]

(ii) If S utters a sentence x literally, then there is a meaning M such that it is true both that S means M by x, and M is one of the meanings of x. Hence, a literal utterance of a sentence can be contrasted with an ironical one. Ironical utterances involve a form of indirect communication, since what the speaker intends to convey is never identical with what he could have said, in the context, by uttering his sentence literally. The speaker intends the difference between what is conveyed and what he could have said to be recognized, and such recognition usually

---

[5] Since one does not always mean something by uttering x when one performs an illocutionary act this is not quite accurate. What is necessary is that one should have the sort of complex intention one has to have to mean something by uttering x. See Chapter 8.

reinforces the force of what is conveyed, making, for instance, a critical remark even more wounding. An ironical utterance of a sentence x, therefore, satisfies the condition that

(6) What the speaker S intends to convey by uttering x is not identical with what he could have said in the context, by uttering x literally.

The type of indirect communication exemplified by an ironical utterance has, of course, to be distinguished in a number of respects from that which is exemplified by hinting and suggesting (see p. 62). The principle differences stem from the fact that the use of, for example:

(7) She has an awful lot of gentlemen visitors.

to hint on a given occasion that she is not nearly as virtuous as she seems in no way precludes its use on that occasion also to state that she is visited by a lot of gentlemen. Indeed, the statement that she is visited by them is obviously meant to supply the main clue to what is hinted. By contrast, if (7) is used ironically, it would simply be an error to suppose that the speaker *states* that she is visited by numerous gentlemen, for his meaning is that few if any of her visitors are gentlemen—males perhaps, but gentlemen no! In spite of this important difference it is illuminating to compare a hint with an ironical utterance; for whereas the former may involve a contrast between something conveyed and what is *said*, the latter involves one between something conveyed and what the speaker could have said by a literal utterance of his sentence in the context.

(a) It is sometimes maintained that sarcasm is not a form of irony because there can hardly be any pretence about the speaker's real meaning.[6] However, even if the last point is granted, sarcasm has a good claim to be classed as a conventionalized form of irony, as can be seen by considering a sarcastic utterance of 'What an *original* thing to do.' This momentarily encourages the hearer to think that he is being praised before he realizes that he is not, and the contrast between what is apparently said and what is conveyed makes what is conveyed all the more wounding to him. Moreover, since the example shows that momentary deception is possible, it can, at the most, be maintained that what is characteristic of sarcasm is

[6] See Muecke (1970), p. 51.

the fact that it is virtually impossible not to detect such deception, since it is conventionally indicated by tone of voice,
manner of utterance, etc.

The effect of sarcasm is usually said to be inversion. This
seems to be correct for a large number of cases, provided that it
is not taken to mean that what is conveyed has to be the con-
tradictory of what could have been said on a literal interpretation of the words used. Often a sarcastic utterance is produced
by stressing some word or phrase, and to grasp what is meant it
is necessary to supply an intuitive 'opposite' for this alone. Thus,
the force of 'That was a *clever* thing to do' is not that it was not a
clever thing to do, but that it was a stupid thing to do. The
point is perhaps most obvious in the case of complex utterances:
'It was *kind* of you to leave me such a *large* share' has to be
distinguished from 'It was *kind* of you to leave me such a large
share'. In the former case what is conveyed is that it was unkind
of you to leave me so small a share, in the latter that you were
unkind to leave me so large a one.

It is clear in outline how the semantic interpretation of a
sentence which is used sarcastically proceeds, since some word
or phrase in the sentence has to be given a reading which, whilst
not one of its normal readings, is systematically related to one
of its normal readings. There is, therefore, no problem in principle in associating a set of truth conditions with a sarcastic
utterance. The effect of sarcasm on illocutionary force is, on the
other hand, not easy to describe; but in general it would seem
to be the case that the range of acts which can be performed by
uttering a sentence sarcastically includes no broad categories,
i.e. expositives, verdictives, exercitives, etc., which are not included in the range which can be performed by uttering it
literally. More specifically, the most noticeable feature of acts
performed by sarcastic utterances of indicatives is that a very
large number of them tend to be behabitives, and it seems possible that a sarcastic utterance always involves an attempt to
criticize, blame, praise, etc., whatever other act is attempted.
At first sight the inclusion of praise is surprising; but it is clear
that an apparently offensive remark which is not really meant
to be offensive can be designed to convey appreciation, just as
an apparently complimentary remark which is not meant to be
complimentary can be designed to convey criticism.

(b) Verbal irony is often much harder to detect than sarcasm, for though there may be linguistic indications that a sentence is being used ironically, there do not have to be any such indications.[7] The sorts of clues that a speaker may give that his utterance is meant to be ironical can be very slight indeed, and it is hardly surprising that verbal irony is often not recognized.

It is probably not sensible to suppose that it is possible to list every type of clue which a speaker might give that an utterance is ironical, but many evidently involve a striking lack of connection between a statement made and the reasons cited in support of it. These may, for instance, not support the statement at all, though they all too clearly support its negation. If Robinson says at an examiners' meeting 'Since he copied his thesis word for word without making a single mistake, he should undoubtedly get the degree. Such accuracy is quite exceptional!', then his meaning is plainly that the student should not be awarded the degree. What Robinson wishes to maintain is the negation of what he apparently states, so the effect of irony in this case is inversion also. In another type of example, a speaker states a more-or-less unanswerable case for drawing a certain conclusion, but then appears to draw it in only a qualified sort of way. To understand what he is conveying it is necessary to remove the apparent qualifications, hedges, etc.[8] In a third type of case the reasons given in support of a particular statement are so patently preposterous that the audience has to suppose that the speaker knows that they are, and expects his audience to see that this is so. But if this is so, then the speaker must expect that his audience will argue that his citing so frivolous a reason in support of his statement shows that he does not really wish to affirm it all. Swift provides us with an amusing example:

But if no other Argument could occur to exclude the *Bench* and the *Bar* from the list of Oratorial Machines, it were sufficient that the Admission of them would overthrow a Number which I was resolved to establish, whatever Argument it might cost me; in imitation of

[7] See Householder (1971), p. 89, for some suggestions.
[8] For example: '. . . when some confessed they owed their greatness and wealth to sodomy or incest; others to the betraying their country or their prince; some to poisoning, more to the perverting of justice in order to destroy the innocent: I hope I may be pardoned if these discoveries inclined me a little to abate of that profound veneration which I am naturally apt to pay to persons of high rank . . .' (*Gulliver's Travels*, 3.8).

that prudent Method observed by many other philosophers and great Clerks, whose chief Art in Division has been to grow fond of some mystical Number . . .

(Introduction to *A Tale of A Tub*.)

In many cases verbal irony involves inversion, or the removal of pretended qualifications, or hedges; but are there other types of case? To avoid confusion, it is important to remember that irony is not always verbal, but can take the form of pretending to agree when one does not, to promise when one does not, and so on.[9]

'Well, these books are all scientific', insisted Tom, glancing at her impatiently. 'This fellow has worked out the whole thing. It's up to us, who are the dominant race, to watch out, or those other races will have control of things.'
'We've got to beat them down' whispered Daisy winking ferociously towards the fervent sun.

(*The Great Gatsby*, Chap. 1.)

Daisy is being ironical, but she certainly is not trying to convey that we have not got to beat them down. On the contrary, she is ironically agreeing with her husband in a way which, in parodying his views, exposes their vacuity. Indeed, as Kierkegaard points out, a common type of irony consists in pretending to be serious when one is not, or even in pretending to be joking when one is not.[10] Cases of this sort should be sharply distinguished from verbal irony. Both types may involve inversion, but the inversion in question is quite different. If I pretend to joke when I am in fact serious, then the intended effect of inversion is to lead the audience to take seriously what was apparently not meant seriously. But in a case of verbal irony, the intended effect is that the audience should conclude that the negation of what is apparently maintained is what is in fact maintained.

[9] Cf. 'In relation to a foolishly inflated wisdom which knows about everything it is ironically correct to go along with it, to be transported by all this knowledge, . . . although through all this the ironist is himself aware that the whole thing is empty and void of content.' (Kierkegaard (1966), p. 266.)
[10] Kierkegaard, (1966) p. 267.

CHAPTER 8

I HAVE argued that the fact that a sentence x has, for example, truth conditions partially determines the nature of the illocutionary acts which can be performed by uttering it literally. Given that x is used literally, and that something is meant be uttering it, then if an illocutionary act is performed, it will be one belonging to a certain range R of illocutionary acts. But the question must now be faced of the nature of the other factors which help to determine which particular act within that range is performed by a literal utterance of x on a given occasion. More generally, it is necessary to ask what type of factor can, in principle, be relevant to the question whether a particular illocutionary act was performed by the literal utterance of a sentence-type. There is, of course, no problem in listing the sorts of things that may be relevant. These include the speaker's intentions; the status of the speaker ('I command . . .'), and that of the hearer ('I request . . .'); the knowledge of the speaker ('I report . . .'), and that of the hearer ('I remind you . . .'); to mention but a few. Indeed, struck by the diverse character of these factors, one might well conclude, as Furberg did,[1] that the unity of the class of illocutionary acts is merely nominal.

Before trying to answer the questions just raised, it is worth making a terminological innovation distinguishing the illocutionary force of an utterance from the illocutionary act performed. One could so use 'illocutionary force' that an utterance could, for example, have the force of a command only if it is a command; but I shall not do so. Instead, I shall so use it that an utterance has the force of a command provided that the speaker is trying to issue a command, even though he may fail to do so. The distinction is prima facie an important one; for whilst illocutionary force in my sense can reasonably be held to be constituted by the speaker's intentions, it is much more doubtful whether in many cases an illocutionary act can.

[1] Furberg (1971), p. 217.

I. SOME GRAMMAR

Certainly, it takes very little reflection to see that we are in no position yet to say what other factors help to determine which illocutionary act has been performed on a given occasion. The sort of conclusion we have been able to establish is that if x is an indicative uttered literally, etc., then the acts which belong to R will be ones which have a certain sort of object. But this is so weak a necessary condition that it does not even distinguish illocutionary from perlocutionary acts, since the report of the perlocution 'I persuaded him that Russell's theory is mistaken' has the same object as does the report of the illocution 'I stated that Russell's theory is mistaken.'

This is not too discouraging, of course, since it is reasonable to hope that it is possible to distinguish verbs which name illocutionary acts from ones which name perlocutionary ones using grammatical criteria. For though both sorts of verb take nominalized sentences as their objects, an illocutionary verb can occur as the main verb in a sentence in the first person present indicative without oddity, whilst this is certainly not generally true of perlocutionary verbs, as the following sentences show:

(1) *a I convince you that you are wrong.
      *b I persuade you that you are wrong.
      *c I frighten you that your family is in danger.

In this connection Vendler's grammatical definition of a performative is of special interest,[2] since the main verb in a performative can, assuming univocality, be taken to be the name of an illocutionary act. Vendler notes that occurring in the first person present indicative without oddity is not a feature peculiar to performative verbs, since 'know', 'believe', 'hope', etc. do also. Moreover, the latter are allergic to continuous tenses just as performative verbs are, and both are container verbs, 'verbs, that is, the object of which is a noun-clause or, in modern terminology, a sentence nominalization of a certain type'.[3] Given these similarities between, for example, 'report' and 'know', there does not seem to be much hope of distinguishing them grammatically. Vendler points out, however, that there is an important difference. If asked 'How long have you known

---

[2] Vendler (1972), Chap. 2.
[3] Vendler (1972), p. 12.

that they are separated?', one can answer 'For years', for instance; but there is no non-deviant answer to the question 'For how long have you reported that they are separated?' On the other hand, whilst the question 'When did you report that you saw him?' has 'At 5 p.m.' as a possible answer, the question 'When did you know that you saw him?' has no comparable answer. It is possible, therefore, to distinguish state verbs like 'know' from achievement verbs like 'report' by the fact that the temporal modifications they admit differ.

Unfortunately, however, as Vendler points out,[4] one cannot define a performative verb as a container verb which is also an achievement verb and which can occur in the present indicative active, since this is true also of such verbs as 'decide', 'realize', and 'discover'. However, Vendler goes on to argue that members of this latter class of verbs cannot occur in the first person present indicative without general indications of scope. Hence, 'I decide to go home' is as it stands somewhat odd, though 'I usually decide to go home when he becomes offensive' is not. Vendler concludes that

performatives belong to the genus of propositional verbs, that is, container verbs corresponding to imperfect nominals, all of which show the symptomatic reluctance towards the progressive form. This genus, however, splits into three main species: (a) performatives, with achievement time-schema and unmodified first person singular present occurrence; (b) the *decide* group, with the same time-schema but no such present occurrence; (c) propositional attitude verbs with the state time-schema.[5]

Clearly, performative verbs are sharply distinguished from perlocutionary ones by Vendler's characterization, just as they are from propositional attitude verbs. But it is less clear that group (b) splits off as cleanly as one would wish. Whilst it is rather unusual for many members of this group to occur in the first person present indicative in an unmodified form, this is certainly not true of all of them. Vendler, indeed, notes that this is so; but argues that in such cases the verb is either functioning as a performative, or a propositional attitude verb:

Realize, for example, appears in the role of a propositional attitude verb in the context *I realize that such and such is the case. Identify* and

---

[4] Vendler (1972), p. 15.
[5] Vendler (1972), p. 16.

recognise, on the other hand, may function as performatives: think of
I hereby identify the accused as the man who . . . or *I hereby recognise the
deputy as the representative of . . .*[6]

These points are well taken; but there are other sentences to
which they apply much less clearly, including the following:

(2)   *a*   I notice that we have strawberries for tea.
      b   I discover that we are being watched.
      c   I guess that it's the big one.
      d   I choose to have the red one.

(2) *a*, for instance, is hardly deviant; yet to ask for how long I
have noticed is no more appropriate than asking for how long I
have promised. So 'notice' is not a propositional attitude verb.
On the other hand, it is a pretty unpromising candidate as a
performative verb, since noticing is a perceptual achievement
which does not involve a public performance.

The examples are difficult ones, and it could be argued that
each of them has a performative employment, though the argument would not be very compelling in some cases. But, this
granted, it is difficult to deny that (2) *d*, for instance, could be
used non-deviantly simply to inform someone of what one
chooses; and so used it would not seem to be any sort of explicit
performative.

These problems apart, Vendler's definition leaves us with no
account of the sorts of factors, sentence-type apart, which determine which illocutionary act, if any, has been performed by the
literal utterance of a sentence. Not of course that his definition
of a performative is meant to constitute such an account, since
he maintains that

the exact nature of the speaker's intention determines the particular
illocutionary force of his utterance. If, for instance, in saying 'I'll be
there' my intention is to cause you to believe or to expect, by means
of your recognition of my intention from these words, that I shall be
there, then what I say is intended to have the force of a statement or
a forecast. If, however, my intention in saying those words is to
entitle you to rely on my going there, then it will have the force of a
promise. If finally, those words are intended to make you fear my
going there . . . then it will be a threat.[7]

[6] Vendler (1972), p. 15.
[7] Vendler (1972), p. 62.

This is indeed plausible, and suggests that a consideration of a recent theory of illocutionary acts, that of Stephen Schiffer,[8] which allots considerable importance to the speaker's intentions, will be profitable.

2. ILLOCUTIONARY ACTS AND INTENTIONS

(i) Schiffer's theory is based on his account of so-called 'speaker's occasion meaning' ('S-meaning'). The form of a report of S-meaning is:[9]

(3) By uttering x S meant that . . .

for example, 'By uttering "It is a pseudo-sentence" Ayer meant that it is neither analytic nor verifiable.' Such a report is a report of a specific claim which the speaker intended to convey to his audience, that is, of something which he maintained, and it should be sharply distinguished from a report of what a speaker meant by x, that is, a report of the form:

(4) By x S meant '. . .'

An example of a report of this sort would be 'By "It is a pseudo sentence" Ayer meant "It is neither analytic nor verifiable." ' This, unlike reports of the form (3), is not a report of a claim made by the speaker. If, for instance, Ayer had written 'If it is a pseudo-sentence, then it is meaningless', and someone had asked what he meant by the protasis, one could reply that he meant 'It is neither analytic nor verifiable', even though Ayer did not claim or maintain that it is neither analytic nor verifiable. Hence, the fact that whilst 'meant' in (3) is followed by a that-clause, in (4) it is followed by an expression in quotes, the function of these being to insulate S from any commitment to what is quoted. Reports of the form (3) and (4) should, in turn, both be distinguished from ones of the form:

(5) x means (in L) '. . .'

These do not report what someone meant by uttering x, nor what he meant by x, but only what someone *could* mean by the literal use of x. Once again, the function of the quotes is to mark the fact that there is no commitment to the truth of the quoted item.

It is important to remember that it must always be possible to say what S meant when giving a report of the form (3); for if

8 See Schiffer (1972), Chap. IV.
9 See Grice (1969), p. 149.

S meant that p, then what he meant was that p. Thus, any case in which it is not possible to say what S meant is not a genuine case of S-meaning.

The point is important because often descriptions of what someone 'meant by doing something' are not descriptions of S-meaning, but simply ones of the purpose with which he did something. If someone asks what Smith meant by turning up dressed like that, then it is probably quite clear that a report of S-meaning is not being requested. But there are many border-line cases; by slamming the door, for instance, someone may wish to make us aware that he is angry, even though it is far from clear that he means that he is angry. An analysis of S-meaning, should at least, set out clearly what has to be taken into consideration when deciding whether this is a case of S-meaning. However, before attempting to give such an analysis one plausible principle is that if S knows that x would produce a certain belief in an audience whatever intentions S has when he utters x, then the case is not one of S-meaning. I agree, therefore, with Grice that Salome could hardly have meant that John the Baptist was dead by displaying his head on a platter,[10] since she must have known that the sight of his head on the platter would lead her audience to conclude that he was dead whatever her intentions in displaying the head were. A connected, but slightly different principle is suggested by Armstrong,[11] who maintains that in a case of S-meaning x must function as a mere sign. Hence, shooting at someone to drive them off one's land is not a case of S-meaning, even though by so doing one makes one's intention that they should leave plain, since shooting at someone is what one does to drive them away, and, hence, it is not just a sign. On the other hand, deliberately shooting just in front of someone as a warning, but not at them, may well be a case of S-meaning, for one shoots only to convey something. This is quite a plausible point, but I shall not pursue it further.

(ii) Schiffer's analysis of S-meaning is fairly complicated. But though I have a number of reservations about it, I will discuss only a few of them before going on to discuss his theory of illocutionary acts. For the latter theory presupposes the analysis

[10] See Grice (1969), p. 170. But Schiffer dissents; see Schiffer (1972), p. 56.
[11] Armstrong (1971), p. 442.

of S-meaning, so that various difficulties which are difficulties for the analysis are also ones for it.

(a) At first sight Schiffer's theory is dauntingly, indeed implausibly, complex; the following is one of his definitions:[12]

S meant that p by (or in) uttering x if S uttered x intending thereby to realize a certain state of affairs E which is (intended by S to be) such that the obtainment of E is sufficient for S and a certain audience A mutually knowing (or believing) that E obtains and that E is conclusive (very good or good) evidence that S uttered x with the primary intention

(1) that there be some ρ such that S's utterance of x causes in A the activated belief that $p/\rho(t)$;

and intending

(2) satisfaction of (1) to be achieved, at least in part, by virtue of A's belief that x is related in a certain way R to the belief that p;

(3) to realize E.

However, ignoring the complexity for a moment, Schiffer's crucial idea is clearly that for S to mean that p by uttering x he must by uttering x intend to produce a state of affairs which is good evidence for A that S intends A to believe that p. In other words, it must be the case that [13]

(6) S intends by uttering x to give A good reason to think that (S intends [A to believe that $\{p\}$])

But though this is necessary it is not sufficient. For may not S intend A to have good reason to think that S intends A to believe that p, but not intend A to think that he intends this? Consider, for instance, a case described by Strawson in which S knows that he is being overlooked by A, and knows that A believes that S does not know that he is being overlooked.[14] Clearly, by arranging bogus evidence that p in a spot where A is bound to see it in the normal course of events, S may intend (i) to give A good reason to think that S intends A to believe that p. But he can hardly be said to mean that p because, as Strawson points out, the fact that he does not intend (ii) A to realize that he has

---

[12] Schiffer (1972), p. 63. There is also a definition of 'S meant that A was to Ψ by (or in) uttering x.'

[13] See Armstrong's illuminating proposal; Armstrong (1971), p. 432. As it stands though it is plainly vulnerable to counterexamples in which the speaker does not intend his intention to be recognized.

[14] Strawson (1964), p. 446.

the intention (i) precludes this from being a case of communication. The same difficulty arises if he intends (ii) A to realize that he has intention (i), but does not intend A to realize that he intends (ii), and so on.[15]

Schiffer proposes to meet these difficulties by introducing the notion of mutual knowledge into his definition of S-meaning. Speaking roughly, S and A mutually know that p if and only if each knows that p, each knows that the other knows that p, each knows that the other knows that he knows that p, and so on. Schiffer maintains that in a genuine case of S-meaning S will intend his utterance to produce a state of affairs which is such that if it obtains (i) S and A mutually know that it obtains, and (ii) S and A mutually know that the fact that it obtains is good evidence that S intends A to believe that p. Clearly, the mutual knowledge conditions are not satisfied in the case described by Strawson, and in the other cases in which S has an intention which he does not intend A to recognize.

(b) Conditions (1) and (2) of Schiffer's definition call for some comment, since it is not entirely clear how some of the difficulties which (1) is designed to deal with differ from those which (2) is. The sort of case that prompted Schiffer to propose (2) is the following:[16]

S, a rather advanced neuro-physiologist, knows that by striking a certain chord on a piano he will emit a sound of a certain frequency which will set off a certain neuro-physiological process in the brain of any person of a certain type which will result in that person's remembering what word he first learned as a child. A, let us suppose, is S's assistant; so the above—along with the fact that A is a person of the relevant type and the fact that S knows on independent grounds what word A first learned—is mutual knowledge between S and A. Finally, suppose that S strikes the relevant chord intending to cause A to remember that 'Gesundheit' was the first word A learned and intending the satisfaction of the mutual knowledge conditions.

He goes on to maintain that this fails to be a case of S-meaning because S's 'utterance' is intended to directly cause A to remember that the first word he learned was 'Gesundheit'. If it was a case of S-meaning, S's 'utterance' would be intended to cause A to remember this in virtue of the fact that there is a certain sort

[15] See Schiffer (1972), p. 18 ff.
[16] Schiffer (1972), p. 52.

of relation between S's striking the chord and the belief that 'Gesundheit' was the first word that A learned, namely, one of association, connection, or correlation. If there had been a connection of this sort between the chord and the fact that the first word A learned was 'Gesundheit', and the speaker had intended A's recognition of this connection to play some part in his having the relevant belief, then it might well have been a case of S-meaning. But as things are, Schiffer argues, it is not.

Whilst more needs to be said about the permissible ways in which x can be related to the belief, it seems clear that Schiffer has put his finger on an important condition. Condition (1), on the other hand, is much more problematical. Its full purport is explained by Schiffer as follows:[17]

> It will be convenient at this point to introduce the following notational device. Let
> 'S intends to produce in A the response r/ρ' = df.
> 'S intends to produce in A the response r for which he intends A to have the reason(s) ρ.'
> If A is intended to have truth-supporting reasons for this response (i.e. his belief), then this will be marked by writing
> $$'\rho(t)'$$

Thus, the meaning of (1) is that there is a truth-supporting reason such that S's uttering x causes A to have the activated belief that p for that reason; and it is a consequence of Schiffer's definition that S must intend the state of affairs he produces to be good evidence that there is such a reason. The sort of case which Schiffer hopes (1) will exclude seems to be[18] one which would arise if it is mutually known by S and A that A has been so conditioned that whenever he hears a certain sound, 'Miouw' produced with a certain intonation, for instance, he thinks that his cat is being tortured. But, according to Schiffer, even if S produces the sound intending the satisfaction of the mutual knowledge conditions, and intending A's recognition of the fact that the sound is related in a certain way to the belief that the cat is being tortured to play some part in getting A to believe this, S does not mean anything by producing the sound.

In the cases which (2) is designed to exclude, the 'utterance'

---

[17] Schiffer (1972), p. 57.
[18] Cf. Schiffer (1972), pp. 55 and 59.

directly causes a certain belief without being correlated with it in any special way, so that the belief is produced whether or not A recognizes S's intentions. On the other hand, in the cases which (1) is designed to exclude the 'utterance' is correlated in a certain way with the belief that p, and A has to see that it is so correlated to have the belief that p. But provided that he sees that x is correlated with the belief that p, A will believe that p whether or not he recognizes the other intentions with which S uttered x. Both sorts of case, therefore, have the feature that there is something about the relation between x and A's belief which would lead A to form that belief if x was uttered, even though he failed to recognize all, or the bulk of, the intentions with which x was uttered. This prompts the question whether at bottom the two sorts of case are all that different.

Certainly, if (2) is to exclude the cases it was designed to exclude, a general restriction on R will have to be that R must not be a relation which holds directly between x and a belief. So that a case in which S intends that it should be just the sound 'Miouw' which makes A believe that his cat is being tortured, which is after all much the most likely case, is already excluded by (2).

The sort of case which Schiffer thinks (1) is needed to exclude would, presumably, be one in which, for example, a sergeant-major having no reason to suppose that Private Jones is in any way abnormal, utters 'Turn right!' with all the appropriate intentions, intending to get Private Jones to turn right, and intending that the fact that 'Turn right!' is related by R to this action to play some part in getting him to perform it.[19] The trouble is that Private Jones is so constituted that he cannot help turning right once he realizes that an 'utterance' is correlated by R with that action, no matter what the speaker's intentions are. However, given that the sergeant-major does not know that Private Jones is so constituted, it is difficult to see why this should not be a case of S-meaning. For since the sergeant-major assumes that Private Jones is normal, he cannot be relying on this peculiar fact about Private Jones's psychology to play any part in getting Private Jones to turn right. If, of course,

---

[19] This case is relevant to Schiffer's proposed analysis of 'By uttering x S meant that p' if he offers, as he does, a similar one of 'By uttering x S meant that A was to Ψ.' See Schiffer (1972), p. 63.

the sergeant-major knows about this fact about Private Jones's psychology, then the situation is less straightforward. But if he is precluded, in this case, from meaning that Private Jones is to turn right by uttering 'Turn right!', this is simply because he cannot be supposed to intend that it should be the satisfaction of the mutual knowledge conditions which gets Private Jones to turn right, since he knows that their satisfaction can play no part in getting him to do this.

There is, therefore, good reason to doubt whether condition (1) is really necessary. That this is so is further supported by the fact that someone who says 'I know that it happened; don't ask me how I know, but I do' means that he knows that it happened. But he can hardly be supposed to intend to provide his audience with good reason to think that there is a truth-supporting reason why it should believe that it happened. It is also worth adding that Private Jones's condition is so remarkable a one, that one might well be sceptical whether it could exist. For it is not supposed to be a certain sound, but the fact that he recognizes that that sound is correlated in a certain way with the action of turning right which causes him to turn right. But if recognition of the correlation, rather than of the sound itself, is the crucial causal factor, it seems that whenever Private Jones recognizes that a sound is correlated with the action of turning right he will turn right. His condition is, indeed, a remarkable one.

Finally, the reason for mentioning activated belief rather than belief, explicitly in (1) and implicitly in (2), is that S may only be reminding A of something that he already believes, so that his aim is not to get A to believe that p, but to get A to have in mind a belief he already has.[20] Of course, trying to get someone to have the activated belief that p does not preclude one from trying to get him to have the belief that p, for one may have to do the latter to do the former.

3. SCHIFFER'S THEORY OF ILLOCUTIONARY ACTS

(i) According to Schiffer, illocutionary acts divide into two classes, the '⊢' class and the '!' class. An act belongs to the '⊢' class only if in performing it S meant that p; and it belongs to the '!' class only if in performing it S meant that A was to ψ.

[20] See Grice (1969), p. 169, and Schiffer (1972), p. 45.

Each of these classes has, Schiffer maintains, a number of sub-divisions: the '⊢' class subdivides into the 'p-identifiable' class, the '$\rho(t)$-identifiable' class, and the 'p-andρ-(t)-identifiable' class; and there are analogous subdivisions of the '!' class, except that the class which corresponds to the p-identifiable class, the 'ψ-identifiable' class is empty.

An act I is a p-identifiable illocutionary act if and only if to perform it a speaker has to mean that p and the belief that p is of a certain specified form F.[21] In other words, if I belongs to this class, not only must the speaker intend to cause A to actively believe that p, etc., but the belief must be of a certain form. An example which Schiffer gives is answering. If by uttering x S was answering A's question, then by uttering x S meant that the answer to A's question was such and such. So that, if by uttering 'Six o'clock' I am answering your question 'What time is it?', I mean that the answer to your question is that it is six o'clock. Other examples of p-identifiable acts are, Schiffer claims, affirming, correcting, denying, and illustrating.

An act I is a $\rho(t)$-identifiable illocutionary act if and only if to perform it S has to utter x intending it to be mutual knowledge between him and A that he uttered x intending A to have the activated belief that $p/\rho(t)$, etc. and $\rho(t)$ is of a certain form.[22] In other words, if I belongs to this class not only must S intend to cause A to actively believe that p, etc., he must also intend A to have a certain sort of truth-supporting reason for his belief (and for it to be mutually known that he so intends). Thus, according to Schiffer, reporting is a $\rho(t)$-identifiable act because in uttering x S is reporting only if by uttering x S means that p, and intends it to be mutual knowledge that he intends part of A's reason for believing that p to be the fact that S himself believes that p on the basis of his own observations. Other acts which belong to this class are, Schiffer claims, assuring, infer-ring, and suggesting.

Obviously, an act is p-and $\rho(t)$-identifiable if and only if it is both p-identifiable and $\rho(t)$-identifiable; members of this class include, on Schiffer's account, apologizing, promising, predict-ing, and thanking. I shall not describe the subdivisions of the '!' class, since they correspond in an obvious way to those of the '⊢'

---

[21] For a fuller account see Schiffer (1972), p. 95.
[22] A fuller account is given by Schiffer (1972), p. 97.

class. Diagrammatically Schiffer represents his conclusions as follows:[23]

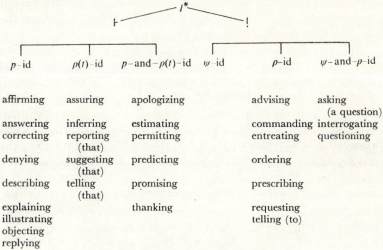

p-id	$p(t)$-id	p-and-$p(t)$-id	ψ-id	p-id	ψ-and-p-id
affirming	assuring	apologizing		advising	asking (a question)
answering	inferring	estimating		commanding	interrogating
correcting	reporting (that)	permitting		entreating	questioning
denying	suggesting (that)	predicting		ordering	
describing	telling (that)	promising		prescribing	
explaining		thanking		requesting	
illustrating				telling (to)	
objecting					
replying					

* ('*I*' designates the class of illocutionary acts)

(iia) One striking difference between the p-identifiable and the $p(t)$-identifiable class is that the analysis of the latter takes us beyond the strict confines of the analysis of S-meaning, since S has to have a separate and additional intention, or, anyway, a special one, i.e. the intention that it be mutual knowledge that he intended A's reason for believing that p to be of a certain sort. And that he does have to have this extra intention is certainly plausible, since it seems unlikely that there is any feature of an actual utterance of, for example, 'They are in retreat', when it is used to make a report, which indicates that S intends A to believe that they are in retreat because S himself believes this having seen them. Instead, it is surely some easily noticeable feature of the context of utterance, the fact that S has returned from the front with mud on his boots, for instance, which, speaking roughly, S intends will provide A with the vital clue to the sort of reason which S intends him to have for believing that they are in retreat. Indeed, if some feature of an utterance of 'They are in retreat' indicated to A what reason he was meant to have for

[23] Schiffer (1972), p. 99.

believing that they are, then, on Schiffer's account, S will come perilously close to meaning that they are in retreat, and I intend you to believe that this is so because . . .

These observations prompt an interesting question about the p-identifiable class, namely what feature of S's utterance of x, in a particular case, indicates that the belief p which S intends A to adopt is of a specific form? Given Schiffer's theory of S-meaning there has to be such a feature, since if S meant that p by uttering x, x has to be related in a certain way R to the belief that p (cf. condition (2)). Lacking an explicit theory of the sort of relations 'R' can range over, it is not possible to say with precision whether any given case violates this condition or not. However, it is surely very implausible to suppose that if I object to the appointment of Joe as cox of the eight by uttering:

(7) He's only got one eye.

my utterance is related in one of the appropriate ways to the belief, which it has to be related to on Schiffer's account, that the fact that he has only got one eye is a reason for not having him as cox. My sentence certainly is not a conventional means of expressing this belief; and though on this occasion I was using it to state an objection, there is nothing to prevent me using it in quite different ways on other occasions. So no feature of the sentence correlates it exclusively with objecting, and hence with the belief in question. Thus, the claim that by uttering (7) I meant that the fact that he has only one eye is a reason for not having him as cox ignores one of the basic insights of Schiffer's analysis of S-meaning, namely, that the utterance must be related in certain ways to the belief which S is trying to get A to adopt.

There is, perhaps, a further reason why, on Schiffer's own theory, one could not mean that the fact that he has only one eye is a reason for not having him as cox by uttering (7) literally. For by uttering (7) literally, if one meant anything, one would surely mean that Joe has only got one eye, and hence one's utterance would be intended to be good evidence that one's primary intention is that A should believe that Joe has only one eye.[24] But in that case, one could not also intend one's utterance to be good evidence that one's *primary* intention is that

---

[24] For the reasons which lead Schiffer to refer to S's primary intention see Schiffer (1972), pp. 60 ff.

A should believe that the fact that Joe has only one eye is a reason for not having him as cox.

It would, therefore, seem to be reasonable to conclude that in at least some of the p-identifiable cases it is not a feature of what is uttered which provides the vital clue that it is being uttered with certain intentions in virtue of which it has a certain illocutionary force, but certain features of the context of utterance. Thus, we have in these cases also to consider intentions which are additional to those involved in meaning something. For instance, if by uttering (7) I object that Joe should not have been made cox, then as well as having those intentions which are necessary to mean that he has only got one eye, I must, as well, have other intentions, whose existence is indicated by features of the context of utterance, in virtue of which what I say has the force of an objection.

(b) If, contrary to the conclusions just argued for, one wishes to maintain, as Schiffer does, that the only intentions relevant to illocutionary force, additional to those which are relevant to S-meaning, are those which indicate what type of reason S has in mind when performing a $\rho(t)$-identifiable act, then it is clear that he will have the greatest difficulty in accounting for many illocutionary acts. Schiffer, for instance, places affirming in the p-identifiable class. This means that to affirm that it is raining (i) there must be some p such that one means that p, and (ii) p must be of some specific form. Yet what can this be? To affirm that p is to give another reason to believe that one believes that p, and can, perhaps, be taken as an expression of one's belief that p. But, surely, to affirm that p is not to mean that one believes that p. Similar remarks apply to maintaining, stating, conceding, and many others. To mention just one of these; by saying 'He's like a Greek god' Sally can agree with Jane's ecstatic comment 'He's divine.' But she can hardly be supposed to mean, in that case, something of the sort that he is like a Greek god, and the fact that he is bears out what Jane says. Schiffer's account goes wrong in these cases by taking features of the context of utterance which are indications of the way in which what is said is intended to be taken, as clues to what is meant.

It is difficult too to see how commissives fit into the scheme. Schiffer places promising in the p-and-$\rho(t)$-identifiable class, so, presumably, he would place the other commissives there. But if *S* has promised to go to the party, what is the truth-supporting reason he intends *A* to have for believing that he will go? *A* may indeed have such a reason, namely, the fact that *S* has promised and is the sort of man who keeps his promises; but *S* surely does not intend *A* to believe that he will go to the party for that reason.

Further problems stem from the requirement that if an act *I* is an illocutionary act, then in performing it one must either mean that p or that *A* is to ψ. For, surely, someone who begs, prays, or even requests to be left alone by uttering 'Leave me alone!' does not mean that *A* is to leave, any more than someone who asks a question means that *A* is to answer. And Schiffer's assignment of most of the acts that can be performed by literal utterance of an imperative to the ρ-identifiable class seems dubious in the light of our earlier discussion of the view that the function of the imperative mood indicator is to indicate that in the speaker's view there is a reason why the audience should perform a certain act (see Chapter 5, Section 3 (ii)).

In view of these problems it seems right to allow that in cases in which in performing an illocutionary act *I S* means something as well as those intentions he must have to mean something, and those which bear on the type of reason *S* intends *A* to have for adopting a certain belief, other intentions may be determinants of illocutionary force. More radically, it seems necessary to allow that there are cases in which an utterance has a certain force even though nothing is meant by *S*. This conclusion suggests that a very radical departure from Schiffer's theory is required. However, I think that many of his basic insights can be incorporated into a satisfactory theory, since it is plausible to suppose that a sophisticated version of the basic pattern (6) is involved in all illocutionary acts.

One final comment: Schiffer's theory, as it stands, is clearly only one of illocutionary force and, hence, only a partial theory of the nature of illocutionary acts. To command, for instance, it is necessary to have the authority to do so. So, in order to give a command by uttering *x* it is not sufficient that by uttering *x* one means that *A* is to ψ, and openly intends *A* to have as his reason for doing so the fact that it is the expressed wish of someone in authority that he should—though this may be sufficient to endow the utterance with the force of a command—since despite one's intentions one may lack the requisite authority.

4. ILLOCUTIONARY FORCE

We cannot rest content with the claim that what an illocutionary act and a case of S-meaning have in common is the fact that

(6) S intends by uttering x to give A good reason to think that (S intends [A to believe that $\{p\}$]).

This would not be a complete characterization in either case. To arrive at such a characterization in the former case, some way of dealing with the problems Schiffer's mutual knowledge condition is designed to deal with must be found, for similar counterexamples to those which show that (6) is not a sufficient condition of the truth of 'By uttering x S meant that p' show that it is not one of the truth of 'By uttering x S performed an illocutionary act.' Secondly, we must both take account of Schiffer's condition (2), which seems to be correct, and also allow features of the context of utterance to provide A with some clue to the force with which x is uttered. Finally, we must say what, apart from S having certain intentions, must be the case, if S is to perform a certain illocutionary act. This final task we will leave until the next section, so that our aim in this one will be to develop a theory of illocutionary force.

(i) *Mutual knowledge*

If Schiffer's notion of mutual knowledge were a satisfactory one, then (6) could be modified, to deal with the problems which led Schiffer to introduce his notion by introducing analogues of his mutual knowledge conditions. However, in view of the problems which emcompass the notion of mutual knowledge, another solution seems preferable.

(a) Schiffer's notion of mutual knowledge was introduced to deal with certain problems with Grice's 1957 analysis of S-meaning which arise from the fact that S may have intentions which he does not intend to be recognized. Grice's original analysis was:

S meant something by uttering x if and only if S uttered x intending,

(i) to produce a response r in an audience A;

(ii) A to recognize S's intention (i);

(iii) A's recognition of S's intention (i) to be part of his reason for producing r.

Grice later (see Grice (1969)) proposed two different ways of dealing with the relevant counterexamples. The first simply adds further conditions to the effect that S intends a relevant lower order intention to be recognized. For example, the counter-example described by Strawson, which we discussed earlier (see p. 133), is dealt with by adding the condition:

(and intending)

(iv) that A recognize S's intention (ii).

But this looks decidedly *ad hoc*; and I agree with Schiffer that, notwithstanding Grice's arguments to the contrary, it is un-satisfactory.[25]

Grice's other proposal is, however, much more intuitive. It consists not of adding more and more conditions stipulating that a lower order intention S has is meant to be recognized, but of requiring, in effect, that S should not intend any of his relevant intentions not to be recognized. More precisely, Grice proposed the addition of the following to his original definition, to yield what he called 'Redefinition IIB'.[26]

there is no inference-element E such that S uttered x intending both (1) that A's determination of r should rely on E and (2) that A should think S to intend that (1) be false.

Schiffer maintains, however, that the addition of this condition fails to exclude the following counterexample: S, who has a terrible voice, sings 'Moon over Miami' intending that A should recognize that he is, and infer therefrom that S intends A to leave the room, so that at least part of A's reason for leaving the room will be his recognition of this intention. But whilst S intends A to *think* that S wants to get rid of him by singing in such a repulsive manner, in fact S intends him to leave simply because he sees that S wants him to do so. In other words, there is a discrepancy between the reason A is meant to think S wants him to have for leaving and the reasons S in fact wants him to have.

Does Redefinition IIB exclude this case then? If we call the belief that S wants A to leave the room 'B', then it is true that S intends (i) A's belief B to be an element in A's practical infer-ence. It is also true that S does not intend A to think that S

---

[25] Schiffer (1972), p. 23.
[26] Grice (1969), p. 159.

intends (i). But it does not follow—as it should if Grice's condition is to exclude this case—that S intends A to think that S intends (i) to be false. As Schiffer comments:[27] 'this example would still be a counterexample if A thought (and was intended to think) that S sang 'Moon over Miami' not caring in the least if S wanted him to leave but simply expecting that a bit of repulsive singing would be more effective.' The problem is that Grice's condition only excludes cases in which S wants A to argue in a certain way and also to think that he is meant not to argue in that way. But in Schiffer's example S merely does not intend A to think that he is meant to argue in a way in which he is meant to. However, this does not show that Grice's proposal cannot be reformulated, only that as it stands it will not do. But instead of pursuing the matter further, Schiffer introduces the notion of mutual knowledge to solve the difficulty.

(b) If '$K_{SA}p$' $=_{df}$ $S \& A$ mutually know that p, then according to Schiffer

$K_{SA}p$ if and only if $K_s p$

$$K_A p$$
$$K_s K_A p$$
$$K_A K_s p$$
$$K_s K_A K_s p$$
$$K_A K_s K_A p$$

.

.

.

But is mutual knowledge defined in this way possible? Schiffer's attempt to explain how it is seems to be constructed with an example in mind which is far from convincing. This is as follows:[28] you and I are seated opposite each other, and on the table between us there is a conspicuous candle. I know that there is a candle on the table; so $K_s p$. Moreover, I know that if a 'normal' person faces an object of a certain size with his eyes open, etc., then he will see it, and I know that you are normal, that you are facing the candle, that your eyes are open, etc.; so $K_s K_A p$. Further, I know that you know the law about normal persons, and that you know that I am normal, that I am facing

---

[27] Schiffer (1972), p. 26.
[28] Schiffer (1972), p. 33.

the candle, that my eyes are open, etc.; so $K_SK_AK_Sp$. What is more, Schiffer urges, there is nothing to stop us going on to construct a further step, and then another, and so on.

Perhaps the most natural objection is that in the circumstances described I surely do not know, for instance, that $K_SK_AK_SK_AK_SK_AK_SK_AK_SK_AK_Sp$, but am, at best, in a position to carry through a piece of reasoning which will have this as its conclusion.[29] Schiffer thinks that much of the force of this objection is removed by noting that there are many things that one knows which have never entered one's head. This is correct, but not clearly to the point. For there are surely many objections to supposing that because someone knows each one of a set of premisses is true, and it is the case that these have a certain consequence q, he knows that q. Yet in Schiffer's example in order to get the regress going it is necessary to assume that because S knows a truth of the form 'All normal persons are ø, and knows one of the form 'A is normal', he knows that A is ø It is also doubtful whether people know statements to be true which they do not understand. But it is far from clear that the result of reiterating 'K_SK_A' more than twenty times is something that most people can understand, let alone that they can construct an argument which has it as conclusion.

Secondly, the supposed law about normal persons is highly questionable. People without any abnormalities (shortsightedness, colour-blindness, etc.) often do not see medium-sized objects which they are facing. No doubt the 'law' could be formulated in a way which referred to factors like attention, set, propensity to daydream, familiarity with the objects in question, etc.; but one would often not know whether the initial conditions of such a law were satisfied or not.

In his general account of the conditions which have to be satisfied for mutual knowledge to obtain Schiffer commits himself to the claim (Thesis 1) that[30]

---

[29] An account of mutual knowledge which seems to me preferable, and which successfully avoids this objection, is given in Lewis (1969), Chap. 2. However, since the knowledge involved is only potential, the account may not serve Schiffer's purpose.

[30] Schiffer (1972), p. 32. Schiffer's symbolic version of the principle is:
i.e. $(x)(p)(Kxp \rightarrow (\exists H)(KxHx \& (y) (Hy \rightarrow Kyp \& Ky(z)$
$(Hz \rightarrow Kzp) \& Ky(z)(Hz \rightarrow Kz(w) (Hw \rightarrow Kwp)) \& Ky(z)$
$(Hz \rightarrow Kz(w) (Hw \rightarrow Kw(v) (Hv \rightarrow Kvp))) \& \ldots$

in general, for any person x and any proposition p, if x knows that p, then there is a property H such that x knows that x is H and such that being H is sufficient for knowing p, being H is sufficient for knowing that being H is sufficient for knowing that p, and so on.

For example, Schiffer argues, all 'normal' people know that snow is white, and know that all 'normal' people know this, and know that all 'normal' people know that all 'normal' people know this, and so on. But the example hardly seems to get off the ground, since it is simply false that all normal people know that snow is white. Many a Pacific islander does not, for instance.

That there are properties like H should not, Schiffer maintains, be surprising, for in general (Thesis 2) if one knows that p, then one knows how one knows; and knowing how one knows can simply be construed as knowing that there is a certain property which is such that to have it is to know that p.[31]

But in such cases, it will be in virtue of knowing that p that one knows that one knows that p because one is H, and so one will know that being H is sufficient for knowing that being H is sufficient for knowing that p; and so on.

This third thesis leads Schiffer to conclude that there are properties H such that for any proposition p, if being H is sufficient for knowing that p, then being H is sufficient for knowing that being H is sufficient for knowing that p. And he goes on to claim that if the three theses just outlined are granted the existence of mutual knowledge in the example involving the candle can easily be accounted for.

However, each of these theses is suspect; indeed, the first seems to be simply false. Someone who knows that the colour of the curtains is chrome yellow, or that a certain note has a certain pitch, or that Everest is the highest mountain, etc., may not know of any property he has the possession of which is sufficient for the possession of the relevant bit of knowledge. A similar comment applies also to the second thesis. Mrs. Jones might know that Mr. Jones is angry, but for all that not know how she knows, that is, not know which feature of his behaviour both makes her believe that he is angry and ensures that her belief is a reliable one.[32] And if Kxp did imply $(\exists H)$ $(KxHx$ & $(y)(Hy\rightarrow$

---

[31] Schiffer (1972), p. 33.
[32] See the Introduction to Phillips-Griffiths (1967).

Kyp & $Ky(z)(Hz{\rightarrow}Kzp)$ ..., it seems that a vicious regress would be involved. For to know that p one would have to know that one was H. But to know that one was H something of the form '$(\exists G)(KxGx$ & $(y)(Gy{\rightarrow}KyHy$ & ...$)$' would have to be true, so that one would have to know that one was G, and so on.

Finally, it seems that there are many properties the possession of which is sufficient for the possession of a certain piece of knowledge which do not satisfy the third thesis. For instance, being told by a reliable eyewitness that p may be sufficient for knowing that p; but it certainly is not true that if one is told by a reliable eyewitness that p, then one knows that to be told by a reliable eyewitness that p is to know that p.

(b) It seems desirable, therefore, not to invoke the concept of mutual knowledge to deal with the difficulties it was designed to deal with. Instead, I propose to adopt the line of thought suggested by Grice and incorporated into his Redefinition IIB. His specific proposal has been shown to be inadequate; but it remains possible that a variation of it will do the trick, namely:

> and it is not the case that there is an inference element E such that S uttered x intending A's determination of r to rely on E, but not intending A to think that he so intends.

In Strawson's counterexample, for instance, A is meant to argue that the fact that S intends him to think that p is indeed a reason for thinking that p; but A is not meant to think that he is to argue in this way. On the contrary, he is intended to think that it is the bogus evidence which is intended to make him believe that p.

The condition thus amended requires that each of S's relevant intentions should be open ones, that is, not ones which he does not intend A to recognize. That this is so is very satisfactory, since counterexamples like Strawson's arise precisely because S has an intention which he does not intend A to recognize. I propose, therefore, to meet the counterexamples which Schiffer's mutual knowledge condition was devised to meet by requiring that all relevant intentions should be open ones.

(ii) A proposal

How then can a modified version of (6) be incorporated into a definition of 'S uttered x with a certain illocutionary force' in a way which secures the result which Schiffer's condition (2) is designed to secure, allows for features of the context of utterance to be determinants of illocutionary force, and secures that the relevant intentions are open ones? This question is difficult, and to simplify the task of answering it I shall, to begin with, only attempt to state a sufficient condition of the truth of '*S* uttered *x* with a certain illocutionary force'. This, broadly speaking, will cover only those cases in which an utterance is an expositive, a verdictive, or a behabitive. If we can succeed in stating a sufficient condition, its extension to cover other cases should not be too difficult.

In the following proposal '$q(p)$' is a proposition which contains 'p'; 'q' may be null, in which case '$q(p)$' is identical with 'p'; whilst 'p' itself stands for the proposition expressed by *x*.

(8) *S* uttered *x* with a certain illocutionary force *if S* uttered *x* openly intending

    (i) to do so;

    (ii) that *x* should be related iconically or conventionally to, or be otherwise appropriately correlated with, the proposition that p;

    (iii) that *A* should recognize *S*'s intentions (i) and (ii);

    (iv) that the fact that *S* uttered *x* openly intending (i), (ii), and (iii), should in the context of utterance *C*, which *S* believes to obtain, provide *A* with reason to think that (*S* intends *A* to think that $q(p)$) because . . . .

This account is, like Schiffer's, very complex. However, the basic pattern of (6) is still discernible; that is, *S* intends by uttering *x* to provide *A* with a reason for thinking that *S* wants him to believe something. The case for stipulating that *S*'s intentions should be open ones has already been argued; and (ii) is meant to exclude the same range of counterexamples as Schiffer's condition (2), on which it is modelled. The reference to the context *C* in (iv) is intended to allow features of *C* both to contribute to the determination of the denotation of '$q(p)$' when '$q(p)$' is not identical with 'p', and to determine, at least partially, the reason which *A* is intended to have for thinking that *S* wants him to think that $q(p)$. Since '$q(p)$' may be identical with 'p', (iv) can cover two different types of case. In the first, in which '$q(p)$' is identical with 'p', *S* intends to provide *A* with a reason for thinking that *S* wants him to believe that p. But in the second, in which '$q(p)$' is not identical with 'p', S may intend, for example, to provide A with a reason for thinking that S wants A to think that the fact that p is an objection to a statement of A's; in this case '$q(p)$' is 'the fact that p is an objection to a statement of A's'. Earlier, I argued that whilst, in the second type of case, S may mean that p he cannot mean that $q(p)$, since what '$q(p)$' stands for is not settled by settling what x is iconically, or conventionally, etc., related to.[33] Some of these points, together with one or two others, are worth commenting on at greater length.

(a) Firstly a small point. There would seem to be no reason why, if (8) is correct, an utterance of x should not, on a given occasion, have more than one illocutionary force.[34] If S, who we see is looking out of the window, utters 'It is raining', then if, as seems likely, he intends that we should believe that it is raining because he, an eyewitness, is of the opinion that it is, then he is telling us that it is raining. But it may also be the case that someone has just asked about the state of the weather, in which case his utterance may have the force of a reply as well.

(b) Schiffer's account of S-meaning has a slightly awkward feature, which is carried over into his explanation of illocutionary force, but which (8) lacks. The trouble stems from the mutual knowledge conditions. For if S and A mutually know that the state of affairs which S intends to produce is good, or conclusive, evidence that S has a certain intention, then it seems that S must have that intention. But it seems doubtful whether S does always intend A to believe what he says; A may be counter-suggestible, for instance. Schiffer discusses such cases at length; but his suggestion that it is only in an attenuated sense that S can be said to mean something in such cases seems to me to be implausible.[35] But if (8) is correct, and S merely has to intend that the fact that he has uttered x with certain intentions should, in the circumstances, provide A with a reason for thinking that S intends A to think that $q(p)$, then S need not in fact intend A to think that $q(p)$. For instance, if a fugitive whom I wish to protect is hiding in the cellar, and I am asked where he

---

[33] See Chapter 8, Section 3 (iib).

[34] It will be recalled that it is not completely clear that this is so on Schiffer's account; see Chapter 8, Section 3 (iia).

[35] Schiffer (1972), p. 68.

is by his pursuers, then by uttering 'He's in the cellar' I may wish to give them reason to think that I intend them to think that he is in the cellar. But in fact I do not intend that they should think this, hoping that they will argue that since I cannot be expected to tell them where the fugitive is, whatever I say is simply meant to mislead. This, incidentally, would not mean that I wanted some of my relevant intentions not to be recognized; though I do suppose that the fugitive's pursuers are likely to assume that I have an ulterior motive. There is no inconsistency in my supposing that the fact that I am speaking about a matter of which I have first hand knowledge, does give an audience a reason to think I intend it to have a certain belief, even though other considerations will make it sceptical.

(c) Condition (iv) calls for a number of comments. A difficulty with (8) apparently arises because of cases in which no special feature of the context of utterance is intended to provide A with a reason for believing that $q(p)$. In such cases S intends that A's reason should simply be the fact that S is trying to get him to believe that $q(p)$.[36] However, (8) can accommodate such cases if (iv) is so understood that if no special feature of the context C is intended to provide A with a reason for believing that $q(p)$, then S intends A to think that S intends A to have as his reason for believing that $q(p)$ the fact that S intends him to believe that $q(p)$. In these cases, (8) reduces to something very like Grice's original definition of S-meaning.

However, these are not the only cases to be considered. For instance, the fact that someone who is a *known* authority on the subject which p is about is trying to get A to believe that p may be meant to provide A with a reason for adopting the belief that p. Hence, the reference to the context of utterance in (iv) in a way which permits it to play a part in determining the reason which A is intended to have for believing that $q(p)$.

That the context C should be able to play such a part is important, for it allows for a systematic connection between C and the reasons A is intended to have—the cases in which C is

---

[36] It is debatable whether there are any such cases. It might be argued that we can count as part of the context such presumptions as that there are many items of general knowledge which people possess, that they are unlikely to try to deceive in matters of no consequence, etc.; and that in cases in which S apparently intends A to think $q(p)$ because S wants him to think it, he tacitly relies on presumptions like these to play *some* part in leading A to think that $q(p)$.

irrelevant we have already discussed. For, in those cases in which C is intended to be a partial determinant of A's reason for thinking that $q(p)$, that reason has to be one which S intends A to see that he is meant to have, by seeing that S uttered x with the intentions (i), (ii), and (iii) in the context C. In other words, some feature of the context of utterance must be intended to indicate to A what sort of reason he is to think S intends him to have; this we might dub the principle of the potential determinability of intended reasons from the context. This might not seem much of a restriction. But given that, in the absence of an overriding motive for doing something, one can intend to do it only if one thinks that there is some chance of realizing one's intention, it is certainly a restriction. If, for instance, S is a *known* authority on the subject which p is about, then he can reasonably expect A to adopt the belief that p because S, who is an authority on such matters, is trying to get him to do so. But S can hardly expect A to adopt the belief that p because a recent discovery, which A can know nothing about, proves conclusively that p. For what features of his utterance, or of the context of utterance, could S expect to provide A with a clue that this is the reason he is intended to have?

(d) If a truth-supporting reason for p is one which provides inductive support for p, then it would be too restrictive to follow Schiffer and require that the reason mentioned in (iv) be a truth-supporting reason. If we are to account for verdictives, then we must allow that one possible reason for believing that p will be that S, who has uttered x, is empowered to make judgements, in certain circumstances, on certain matters of fact or of value, etc., and that the circumstances, etc. are appropriate. If S really is so empowered, the circumstances are appropriate, etc., then A will have not merely a good but a conclusive reason for believing that p, since it will now be the case that p because of S's judgement to that effect. It might be argued that in cases like this, sometimes anyway, it is clearly not S's intention to provide some audience with a reason for thinking something. A judge, for instance, is concerned to sentence the prisoner, and not to produce a belief in an audience. I am not convinced that doing the former thing does not involve doing the latter; certainly, in the absence of an audience it would be pointless. But if necessary, (8) could be amended to allow, for instance, that the judge intends that what he does should, in the circumstances, bring it about that the prisoner goes to prison for seven years.

It remains possible that some restriction on the range of relevant reasons is still required. But if features of C are meant to determine the reason A is intended to have, then it seems that an account of the features which are relevant to C, which I attempt to sketch later, will automatically yield the desired restriction.

(e) If attention is restricted to cases in which '$q(p)$' is identical with 'p', and in which features of C are meant to indicate to A which reason he is intended to have for believing that p, then the resulting class seems to be roughly co-extensive with Schiffer's $\rho(t)$-identifiable class. In other words, members of this class can have the force of a report, or of testimony, or of a confession, etc. Interestingly, if a report of the form 'S uttered x with force F' is true in such a case, then so is one of the form 'By uttering x S meant something.' This suggests that the class of cases in which S means something by uttering x is a sub-class of those in which he utters x with a certain force. This is fairly intuitive. For if 'V' ranges over verbs of illocutionary force, it is not always the case that a report of the form 'By uttering x S V'd that p' implies the corresponding report 'By uttering x S meant that p.' For instance, let 'V' be 'estimate', or 'suggest', or 'conjecture'.

(f) When '$q(p)$' is not identical with 'p', it is the fact that S uttered x with the intentions (i) and (ii) and (iii) in the context C which is meant to provide A with evidence that it is a certain proposition $q(p)$ involving p, rather than some other proposition, which S wants him to think that S wants him to believe. In other words, some feature of the context of utterance must be intended to provide A with a clue to the relevant value of '$—(p)$'. Given that this is so, it is easy to see how S could expect A to see that what he intended A to believe was that the answer to his question is that it is raining, if A had just asked whether it is raining, and S had uttered 'Yes'. But S could hardly expect A to see that what he intended A to believe, in the same circumstances, was that it is raining because the wind is in the south, the barometer is falling, it is April, etc.

The class of cases in which '$q(p)$' is not identical with 'p' overlaps Schiffer's p-identifiable class to a considerable extent. In other words, members of this class can have the force of a denial, an objection, a protest, etc. But (8) does not require that if by uttering 'He's only got one eye' S is objecting to the choice of Smith as look-out, then by uttering his sentence S *means* (i) that the fact that Smith has got only one eye is a reason for not choosing him as look-out. Provided that S intends that his utterance should, in the circumstances, provide A with a reason to think that S wants A to believe (i), then it may be an objection; even though S does not *mean* (i).

The fact that according to (8) S's meaning that $q(p)$ is not a necessary condition of S's intending to provide A with reason to think that S wants him to believe that $q(p)$ makes it relatively easy to account for cases in which the utterance of a sentence has the force of a conjecture or a postulation, even though nothing is meant by uttering the sentence. For instance, there seems to be no reason why the fact that someone uttered x with certain intentions, in certain circumstances, should not be meant to give A reason to believe that S was of the opinion that p's truth would be a possible explanation of something, so that the utterance constitutes a conjecture, even though S meant nothing by uttering x.

(*iii*) *Extending the proposal*

It will be recalled that (8) only states a sufficient condition for the truth of 'S uttered x with a certain illocutionary force.' This was designed to cover cases in which an utterance has the force of an expositive, a verdictive, or a behabitive. If (8) is correct, or substantially so, then its extension to cover exercitives, questions, commissives, etc. should not be too difficult. There seems to be no reason, for instance, why S should not sometimes intend x to be 'related iconically, or conventionally to, or be otherwise appropriately correlated with' a directive, or a question, or a commissive, etc. If this is so, then we can readily allow for the possibility that S may intend the fact that he uttered x with the intentions he did to give A good reason to comply with a certain directive (or to think that S wants him to comply); or good reason to think that S wants him to answer a certain question; or good reason to think that S will himself conform with a certain commissive, and so on. This permits the generalization of (8) in an obvious way so that it applies to such acts as ordering, asking, and pledging.

(9) S uttered x with a certain illocutionary force if and only if S uttered x openly intending
   (i) to do so;
   (ii) that x should be related iconically or conventionally to, or be otherwise appropriately correlated with

$$\left(\begin{array}{l} \text{the proposition that } p \\ \text{the directive } D \\ \text{the question } Q \\ \text{the commissive } C \\ \quad . \\ \quad . \end{array}\right)$$

   (iii) that A should recognize S's intentions (i) and (ii);
   (iv) that the fact that S uttered x openly intending (i), (ii), and (iii) should in the context of utterance C, which S believes to obtain, provide A with reason to think that

$$\left(\begin{array}{l} (S \text{ intends } A \text{ to think that } q(p)) \\ (S \text{ wants that}) \text{ } (A \text{ should comply} \\ \quad \text{with } D) \\ (S \text{ wants that}) \text{ } (A \text{ should answer } Q) \\ (S \text{ will comply with } C) \\ \quad . \\ \quad . \end{array}\right) \text{ because...}$$

The choices permitted by (iv) are related in the obvious way to the corresponding ones permitted by (ii); the first to the first, the second to the second, and so on. Bracketed elements which are italicized are optional. Accordingly, line two of (iv) allows for two possible cases. In the first, which is appropriate for orders, commands, etc. and in which the italicized element is omitted, S intends to provide A with reason to think that A should comply with D. But in the second, in which the italicized element is included and which is appropriate for requests, entreaties, etc., S intends only to provide A with reason to think that S wants him to comply with D. If necessary, further choices could be made available.

5. ILLOCUTIONARY ACTS

A theory of illocutionary force is, it was observed, only a partial

theory of illocutionary acts, since what illocutionary act someone performs does not usually depend only on the intentions
with which he uttered something. What then, apart from S's
having certain intentions, is necessary for him to perform an
illocutionary act?

An obvious suggestion is that one thing which is necessary is
that C should be as S believes it to be. If, for instance, S believes
himself to be in authority over A, then for his utterance to
actually be a command, rather than one which merely has the
force of a command, he really must be in a position of authority
over A. If S believes himself to have been in a position to observe
that p, then for his utterance to be a report, instead of one which
merely has the force of a report, he must actually have been in a
position to observe this; and so on. However, in cases in which S
is not relying on any feature of C to provide A with a reason for
believing something, it plainly is not necessary for an utterance
which has a certain illocutionary force to constitute the corresponding act that C should be as S believes it to be. In such cases
C is irrelevant; and it seems that what is necessary for S to perform a certain illocutionary act is simply that A should recognize
that S openly intends (iv). In other words, in this category of
cases it is necessary for S to achieve what Austin called 'uptake',
i.e. to get A to see what he is trying to do.[37] It would be nice if, in
cases in which C is relevant, it is never necessary to secure uptake, since we would then have a clear way of distinguishing
cases in which it is from ones in which it is not. Unfortunately,
though there are many cases in which C is relevant in which it is
not necessary to secure uptake, there are a lot in which it is. It is
doubtful, for instance, whether someone can be said to have
given us a report, if he failed to get us to see that that is what he
was trying to do. Still, it seems clear that if S utters x with a certain illocutionary force then for him to perform the corresponding illocutionary act it is additionally necessary in certain cases
that he achieves uptake; in others that C should be as he believes
it is; and in others that he should both achieve uptake and that
C should be as he thinks it is. What remains unclear is why
sometimes when C is relevant it is also necessary to secure uptake, whilst sometimes it is not.

---

[37] Austin (1962), p. 116.

(i) Relevant circumstances

The conclusion just reached is, of course, far from informative in the absence of an account of what can be a relevant feature of the context *C*, and what not. To give a fully comprehensive account of the nature of such relevant features is not easy, since the principles which determine which features are relevant to expositives and verdictives do not seem to be very precise. However, a survey of relevant features shows without doubt that systematic principles are involved, and an account of what these are completes my account of the nature of an illocutionary act. In what follows I shall first describe the contextual features relevant to expositives and verdictives, and then go on to attempt to discover the general principles in virtue of which they are relevant.

To begin with, one important type of feature plainly concerns *S*'s degree of commitment to *p*. These features constitute what I shall call the dimension of commitment. Clearly, if *S* asserts, maintains, or concludes that *p*, or informs us, or assures us, that *p*, etc., etc., he thereby commits himself unreservedly to the truth of *p*. Similarly, if in saying that *p* someone is objecting, or replying, or illustrating a point, etc., then he is also committed to the truth of *p*. Whilst, to mention a handful of verdictives, to place *X* first is to commit oneself to the truth of '*X* is first', just as to analyse *X* as *Y*, describe *X* as *Y*, or identify *X* as *Y* is to commit oneself to the truth of '*X* is *Y*.'

These are all cases in which *S*'s commitment is full-blooded. But a commitment may be less than full-blooded and, exceptionally, there may be no commitment at all. A suggestion, in the sense in which suggestion is related to a proposal, but not in the sense in which a suggestion involves a kind of indirect communication, commits *S* to no more than the possibility, perhaps with some degree of probability, of the truth of *p*. An interesting group of acts which commit *S* less than full-bloodedly includes estimating (that), calculating (that), and diagnosing. That the speaker's commitment is not full-blooded is shown by the fact that whilst there is an air of paradox about 'I report that *p*, but possibly not-*p*', and 'I identify *X* as *Y*, but perhaps *X* is not *Y*', there is nothing in the least paradoxical about 'I calculate that *p*, but possibly not-*p*', and 'I diagnose *X* as *Y*, but perhaps it isn't'. Since calculations may be rough and proceed from dubious assumptions, whilst diagnoses may be just plain difficult, it is perhaps not surprising that commitment is not unreserved in such cases. Finally, as a limiting case, there may be no commitment at all. To postulate that p is not to put forward p with a very low degree of commitment, but simply to make it clear that without commitment to its truth one is going to argue as if p were true.

In claiming that the extent of the speaker's commitment is relevant to the determination of illocutionary force I am in agreement with Furberg.[38] However, as I see it, the degree of commitment marked by a verb of illocutionary force is either full-blooded, or positive but less than full-blooded, or non-existent. Finer distinctions can, of course, be made within the middle category, but verbs of illocutionary force are not used to mark them. By contrast Furberg argues that there is a continuum of degrees of commitment:[39] 'I have suggested that utterances of a certain discourse can be ordered in a scale with verbally and non-verbally unguarded utterances at the top and utterances merely suggesting a possibility at the bottom.' As an example of an utterance at the bottom of the scale, Furberg cites (i) 'X may be Y',[40] which he seems sometimes not to distinguish clearly from (ii) 'Possibly, X is Y.'[41] It is indeed plausible to suppose that an utterance of (ii) does not commit the speaker full-bloodedly to the truth of 'X is Y', since the role of the sentence-adverb in (ii) is to indicate that it is only in his view that it is possible that X is Y. But if this makes an assertion of (ii) a hedged one, then an assertion of (i) is not also hedged, since to assert (i) is to assert, without qualification or reservation, that it is possible that X is Y.

It is, admittedly, undeniable that 'possibly' in (ii) is a degree-showing device, though 'may' in (i) is not. But 'possibly' contrasts with 'certainly', 'probably', 'very likely', 'just possibly', etc., and this system of devices to mark the speaker's degree of confidence in p in cases in which he does not wish to commit himself to it unreservedly seems to be quite separate from the

---

[38] Furberg (1971), pp. 219 ff.
[39] Furberg (1971), p. 245.
[40] Furberg (1971), p. 247.
[41] See, for instance, Furberg (1971), p. 231.

system of verbs of illocutionary force. None of the following, for instance, is tautological:

(10) I $\left\{\begin{array}{l}\text{estimate}\\ \text{calculate}\\ \text{diagnose}\end{array}\right\}$ that $\left\{\begin{array}{l}\text{almost certainly}\\ \text{very probably}\\ \text{quite likely}\\ \text{possibly}\end{array}\right\}$ X is Y.

Indeed, the function of the sentence-adverbs seems to be precisely to indicate the speaker's degree of confidence in his estimate, etc., so that there is no need to have a 'scale' of verbs of illocutionary force as well to do this, making finer and finer distinctions within the category of cases in which the speaker's commitment is less than full-blooded. We may also note that when a verb of illocutionary force 'V' has a corresponding sentence-adverb 'A', 'I V that p' is not generally equivalent to 'A,p'; 'I report that they will come' is not even roughly synonymous with 'Reportedly, they will come.'

A second type of relevant feature concerns the sort of ground that S has for committing himself to p, to whatever degree he is committed to p. These features constitute what I shall call the domain of evidence. They are ones which determine the evidential worth of what S says in various ways, the link between ground and evidential worth being, of course, that the latter is directly dependent on the former. If, for instance, S is in a position to observe the state of the weather, then the fact that he says that it is raining is, assuming sincerity, a good reason for believing that it is raining oneself. But if, by contrast, S having estimated by eye the time it will take a distant cloud to reach the spot where he is standing announces that it will rain in ten minutes, his estimate will be treated with the caution that something so rough and ready deserves to be.

Various sub-divisions of this second category may be made. In one set of cases S is, or was, in a position which makes him an especially reliable source of information on certain matters either because they concern events which he observed at first hand, or because they directly concern himself. If, for example, he was an eyewitness of certain events, or at least in a position to obtain at first hand reliable information about them, then he is in a position to give us a report about them, or inform us about them, or even to describe or identify certain things for us. If, on the other hand, the subject matter concerns things which

S himself thought, intended, or did, etc., on which subjects what *S* says has, assuming sincerity, an especial authority, then not only is he in a position to tell us certain things, or inform us about them, but he can also admit (in one sense) that they happened, or, if his acts are censurable, confess that they did.

Another set of cases is concerned with the 'procedures' followed by *S* which have led him to commit himself to *p*, though perhaps only qualifiedly. Often these will be cases in which *S* is not in a position to answer the question whether *p* directly on the basis of present or past observation, or from personal knowledge. He may, for instance, have concluded that *p* on the basis of certain observations made, though the connection between them and his conclusion may be far from simple. Or it may be that calculations, diagnostic procedures, etc. had to be used, so that what *S* says has to be taken as the report of the result of such calculations, or diagnoses, etc.

A third set of cases, which overlap the previous two in various ways, concern the authority of the speaker. The kind of authority that is relevant is not that which can be conferred by an authority-conferring rule (e.g. 'I hereby empower you to serve as a magistrate'), but that possessed by an expert in a certain field. The fact that such an expert, after examination, has told me that my painting is indeed a Dufy gives me much more of a reason for thinking that it is, than does the fact that my friendly neighbourhood antique-shop owner said that it was. Of course, experts who make no observations are useless, and an expert will probably have to make use of various diagnostic procedures also, so the fact that the speaker is an authority is only going to be of interest if he is, or was, in a position to observe certain things, etc. Nevertheless, the fact that he is an authority is in such circumstances a different, but relevant, consideration from the others mentioned to date.

Cases in which we are dealing with pronouncements of authorities appointed to decide certain matters—judges, umpires, referees, etc.—pose a dilemma. If we were concerned simply with the ways in which what *S* says when he says that *p* furnish, or fail to furnish, *A* with a reason for believing that *p*, then we could argue that the fact that *S* is an authority appointed to decide on certain matters is a further relevant feature belonging to the dimension of evidence. For example, one who has heard the umpire give the batsman out has a very good reason for thinking that the batsman is out. However, it seems to me preferable to restrict relevant features belonging to the second dimension to ones which concern the sort of *ground* S has for committing himself to p, and to treat those factors which make what S says authoritative, whatever his ground, separately. If nothing else, we avoid grouping together very different sorts of considerations by doing so.

A third type of relevant feature concerns what I call the dimension of assessment. What this involves can best be illustrated by considering a number of examples. If, for instance, S defines X as Y, the fact that he is proposing a definition is not only relevant to his degree of commitment to the truth of 'X is Y', but is also crucially relevant to the way in which his claim is to be assessed. Since what he is proposing is a definition, what he says will not be acceptable simply because it is true that X is Y; additionally, it must, at least, be the case that being Y is necessary and sufficient for being X. Because what S says is intended to be a definition it can be criticized in various ways in which it could not have been had it been a simple assertion. Similar remarks apply to analysing, and even characterizing. Someone who says that he characterizes X's work by its patient attention to detail is not merely committed to the claim that X pays patient attention to detail; he is also claiming that this is characteristic of X's work.

In essence the dimension of assessment is concerned with the relevant ways in which what S says can be supported or criticized. It seems appropriate, therefore, to treat the fact that S is appointed to decide authoritatively on certain matters as one which is relevant to the assessment of what he says when he pronounces authoritatively on these matters. If, for instance, S in his official capacity mistakenly places X first, then X will indeed receive the prize, unless a procedure for appealing against mistaken decisions exists. If it does, then the appropriate thing to do is to appeal against S's decision rather than try to get him to change it by argument about what in fact really happened. Whereas if what S had said had merely been an assertion, argument would have been appropriate, and talk of an appeal a joke.

Fourthly, and finally, we turn to a rather humdrum dimension, which is nevertheless of considerable importance, a discourse-placing dimension. Features which belong to this dimension indicate how what one says is meant to fit into a wider discourse, i.e. how it relates to other speech acts either of A or of S himself. Whether what S says is intended as an illustration of, or an objection to, something A has said is obviously important, since A's belief that S has the former intention, when he in fact has the latter, can lead to very serious misunderstanding. Similarly, whether something is a reply or an interpolated comment can make a great deal of difference; interpolated comments are often irrelevant to the main topic of a discourse in a way in which replies to questions plainly are not. Together with objecting and illustrating we can group answering, denying, conceding, and rejoining; whilst with interposing we can group interjecting.

(ii) Why relevant circumstances are relevant

Even restricting ourselves to expositives and verdictives it is unlikely that we have succeeded in listing all the relevant contextual features, and Furberg is clearly right to stress their heterogeneity. However, it is certainly not necessary to conclude that what we are dealing with is a somewhat arbitrarily chosen rag-bag of features, and that it is not possible to say why these features are the relevant ones. To have to conclude that would mean that once we had made a list of features we could do nothing more than stare blankly at it and exclaim about its peculiarity. But we can do better than that.

To begin with, the features are ones which, in any given case, it is reasonable to expect the speaker to know whether they obtain or not. He can be expected to know, that is, whether he was an eyewitness, whether he is empowered to decide certain things, whether what he says is a conclusion, and whether what he says is intended to illustrate a certain point, or to be an objection to it, etc. Of course, a person cannot always remember whether he witnessed something, so the expectation that he can may be defeated. But the more recent the incident, the greater the likelihood that a person can remember; and it seems a fair assumption that if someone can remember something, it is likely that he is aware that he does—which is not to say that it is a logical truth that if someone remembers that p, then he is aware that he so remembers. By contrast, there are many matters which one cannot expect an arbitrarily chosen speaker, in *any* given case, to have an opinion about, the date of the spring tides this year for instance, and such matters do not seem ever to be determinants of illocutionary force.

Secondly, the relevant features tend to be concerned with relatively 'objective' factors, and to involve as little as possible the speaker's substantive opinions. For instance, a relevant feature of the context of Smith's utterance of 'Three people were killed in the accident' could be the fact that he witnessed the accident, but his opinions about accidents in general, or the causes of this particular one, etc. are not further relevant features. But why not? It is not as though the speaker's beliefs are always totally irrelevant to the illocutionary force of his utterance. He can hardly answer a question, for instance, unless he believes that he was asked one.

It is prima facie plausible to suppose that there has to be a principled limit on what can count as part of the relevant context, otherwise it would inexorably unfold to include everything. But if the speaker's aim is to bring about a certain effect in an audience, which effect he intends to produce by doing something in certain circumstances, he would have very little chance of succeeding if the relevant features of the circumstances could be anything whatsoever. For the chance that his audience would light on the right feature would in that case be exceedingly small. So the irrelevance of the vast majority of *S*'s beliefs is hardly surprising. If any one of them could be relevant, then it is very unlikely that the speaker would guess which one was. Additionally, if any belief whatsoever could be relevant in each case, it is difficult to see how there could be any systematic way of marking and classifying the ways in which it was relevant. Still the fact remains that some beliefs have a bearing on illocutionary force, though most do not, and we have not explained why this is so.

The form which such an explanation must take can, perhaps, be sketched as follows. One would not expect a method, the uttering of an indicative with appropriate intentions, which enabled the communication of a speaker's belief to another, to assume that intended audiences already possess the very information which the method enabled the speaker to communicate. Suppose, for instance, that *S* believes that it is raining, and wanting to tell A of this utters 'It is raining' with the appropriate intentions. His doing so would be pointless, unless it was possible for him to assume that A does not already know that he believes this. What is true of S's belief that it is raining is obviously true of any other belief that he has. So that if there is to be a method of communicating beliefs to another, viz. the utterance of an indicative with an appropriate intention, then it must be the case, if its employment is to have any point, that on each occasion on which S tries to communicate a belief by means of it he need not assume that A already knows that he (S) has that belief. We cannot, of course, move from this conclusion to the further conclusion that on each occasion on which S tries to communicate a belief in this way he need not assume that A has any beliefs at all about his (S's) beliefs. The fallacy involved would be a crude one, and the conclusion is plainly false. However, if the method is a *general* one, enabling the communication of any belief by a member of a linguistic community to any other, the method would be of maximal utility if a speaker's employment of it was compatible with the weakest possible assumptions about the beliefs which his audience has about the speaker's beliefs. For speakers often know very little about their intended audience, and vice versa; so the less the speaker can assume his audience to know about his beliefs, the less likely is their relative ignorance about each other's beliefs to be a barrier to communication. So, if the method is a general one, its utility would be greatest if the success of the communicative act depended as little as possible on the audience's knowledge of the speaker's beliefs. These we can describe in general and not very informative terms as those which the audience must suppose the speaker to have to suppose that he is making use of the method. Such beliefs may be surprisingly numerous, but nevertheless they will constitute a very small proportion of the beliefs the speaker has.

It is, incidentally, worth noting that the fact that there is a good chance that S knows which relevant features are present means that intended force is likely to be a good guide to the actual illocutionary act performed. For if S believes that certain relevant features are present, then they probably are. There are, of course, always problems of sincerity, since S may pretend to believe things which he does not. However, the fact that, problems of sincerity apart, intended force is likely to be a good guide to the actual act performed must facilitate the introduction and use of explicit force indicators.

Unfortunately, none of this tells us why the factors isolated are important and worth taking systematic account of. However, their importance becomes clear if we imagine the plight of A in the following situation. He knows that S has uttered a sentence with a set of intentions of the form (8), and knows moreover what possible state of affairs has to exist for S's sentence to express a true proposition. However, he does not know either what relevant set of contextual features is believed by S to exist, or does indeed exist. In other words, he knows what proposition S's words express—and thus in one sense knows what S says[42]—and knows that S is probably trying to get him to modify his beliefs or expectations in certain ways. But in ignorance of the relevant contextual features he is quite unable to decide how he is intended to modify his beliefs, and whether he should indeed do so. Hence, his capacity to respond appropriately to S's utterance will be severely diminished, and he will wish, therefore, to discover how he is meant to respond and whether he should. It may, of course, be possible for him to ask a number of appropriate questions, but to accept an utterance of S's as a reply he has to know the sort of thing which in the imagined case he is in doubt about, so its importance resurfaces at a different point.

Now if A could take it for granted that S's utterance expressed a belief to which S was unreservedly committed, then one major uncertainty would be resolved, and A could at least add to his stock of beliefs the belief that S has a certain belief. This, moreover, is the sort of belief which it can be well worth one's while to have; in a bargaining situation, for instance, it could be very valuable. However, A cannot just assume full-blooded commitment on S's part. He knows that there are many matters about which he himself holds opinions which are extremely tentative, and has no reason to suppose that S is any different in this respect. And since the fact that S is not fully committed to p may be an excellent reason for not committing himself to p, A will naturally be anxious to know how committed S is.

Unfortunately, even if A knows that S is fully committed, it

[42] Austin (1962), p. 150.

may be quite unclear to him whether he should adopt S's belief. Much depends on the ground S has for believing what he does believe. So if one important question concerns the degree of S's commitment, another concerns the reasons he has for being committed to that degree. The more A knows about these, the better the position he is in to decide whether to believe what S believes.

If the desirability of A's knowing where to 'place' S's utterance on the dimension of evidence is clear, his reason for being interested in the dimension of assessment is perhaps less clear. But since what kind of evidence is relevant depends on what mode of assessment is appropriate, the third dimension must be important if the second is. This apart there are a number of reasons why A should wish to avoid misunderstandings which involve this dimension. For example, to mistake an authoritative pronouncement for a prediction may lead to a quite inappropriate and time-wasting response, namely, trying to show that things will not in fact turn out as predicted. Or, to take a different sort of case, if someone fails to see that S is analysing X as Y, and not merely saying that X is Y, then he will very probably refrain from deploying a number of relevant critical or supporting arguments. And if he is arguing with, or tutoring, S, then he will not want to do that! A's interest in knowing how S's utterance is related to other speech acts of S or of himself is of a similar nature. Conversations take many twists and turns, and serious misunderstandings arise from failures to realize what is an incidental remark, what not, what is meant to be a reply to A's question, what an illustration of his point, and so on.

So far we have looked at things only from the point of view of A, to try to see what features of the context of S's utterance would be of interest to him when considering how, if at all, he should modify his beliefs and opinions in the light of that utterance. However, if we adopt S's viewpoint and suppose him to wish to communicate something to A, then we must also suppose him to wish to furnish A with some reason for modifying his beliefs and opinions. Given that this is so, it is not difficult to see why he should think that he has no chance of doing this unless (i) A knows what possible state of affairs has to obtain for S's sentence to express a true proposition, and (ii) A believes that certain relevant contextual features obtain. He will, for instance, wish A to believe that he is unreservedly committed to p if he is, since if A does not believe that he is then he will be unlikely to suppose that S is trying to get him to believe that p, unless he also supposes that S is insincere, in which case A is unlikely to believe S anyway. S will also wish A to have an appropriate belief about the sort of grounds he (S) has for believing that p, since it is unlikely that the mere fact that S is trying to get him to believe something will lead him to believe it. And it is easy to see why S should wish A to know how his utterance is meant to be assessed, and how it is meant to relate to other utterances in the discourse. So if S has an interest in communicating something to A, then he will have an interest in getting A to think that certain contextual features obtain; and if he is sincere, this interest will coincide with an interest in their actually obtaining.

Reverting to Austin's terminology, we can say that someone understands S's locution if, given that S has uttered a sentence x, he knows what possible state of affairs has to obtain for x to express a truth. We can then describe in general terms the nature of relevant contextual features as follows: they are ones which enable an audience to respond in the way intended to a locution produced by a speaker with an appropriate set of intentions of the form (8)—the intended response being, of course, the formation of the belief that $q(p)$. This description has, however to be qualified in two ways in the light of previous discussion. Firstly, the features have to be ones which there is a good chance, in any given case, of S's knowing whether they obtain or not. Secondly, the features must be relatively objective, i.e. ones such that there is a good chance, in any given case, that A will be able to detect their presence or absence.

If one were to try to design a system which enabled an arbitrarily chosen person to communicate a very wide range of beliefs to any other member of his linguistic community by *doing* something, one could not object to features of the context being relevant on the ground that their being so would tend to inhibit the communication of an arbitrary belief by one person to another, provided that they were ones which there was a good chance of S's knowing whether they obtained, and of A's being able to find out whether they did. On the other hand it might seem to be an imperfection of one's design that such features had to be treated as features of the context. Is it really clear that they have to be treated as contextual? Suppose, for example, that to inform someone who understood a language L that the enemy are in flight one could utter a specific sentence x_j of L in circumstances C. Ought it not to be possible to make explicit the fact that circumstances C are relevant by uttering a further sentence x_k to say that they are? And if this is possible, it would seen that one could inform A that the enemy is in flight by uttering x_k and then x_j, instead of uttering x_j in circumstances C. For example: let x_j be 'The enemy are in flight', C consist in the fact that S has just returned from the front, and x_k be 'I have just returned from the front.' The questions then are, firstly, whether, granted that one could inform someone that the enemy are in flight by uttering x_j in circumstances C, one could not also do this in a completely explicit way by first uttering x_k and then x_j? And, secondly, whether if this is possible, the fact that it is shows that such features are not essentially contextual at all?

Now one undoubtedly can inform someone that the enemy is in flight by first uttering x_k and then x_j. But in doing so one would not succeed in making every feature of one's context explicit, since one has, in effect, enlarged the context. Those features in virtue of which the utterance of x_k itself counts as a report have not been made explicit. We could, of course, do so in the way in which we did before. But in doing so we will have to introduce a third sentence whose relevant contextual features of utterance will not have been made explicit, and so on. Clearly, the goal of complete explicitness cannot be achieved in this way, though nothing has been said which shows that it cannot be achieved in any given case, only that it cannot be achieved in all. A point to which I return later.

It might be argued that the existence of explicit performatives means that there is no reason why complete explicitness should not be achieved in all cases, for is it not always possible to make force explicit by uttering the relevant explicit performative? I, however, am committed to denying this, since I argued earlier (see p. 61) that it is not always possible to make illocutionary force explicit by prefixing a performative prefix to one's utterance, even if we put on one side, as special cases, such indirect speech acts as hinting, suggesting, and the like. One might, for instance, illustrate someone's claim that Smith is a brilliant bat by saying that he scored a century against Australia, but there is no explicit performative one can use to do this.

But even if I am wrong, and illocutionary force can always be made explicit in either one, or both, of these ways, it certainly would not follow that the features in question are not essentially contextual. Suppose that it was always possible to make force explicit in the first way described. Now an important point is that it is not the fact that something was said by uttering x_k, but the fact that what was said was true which places the speaker in a position to give a report by uttering x_j. And since the truth of the claim made by uttering x_k guarantees the presence of C, we can hardly take ourselves to have described a way of making its presence irrelevant. Equally, if it were always possible to make illocutionary force explicit by means of an explicit performative, it would not follow that contextual features are not relevant. On the contrary, if one can report that the enemy is in flight by uttering x_j only if a certain sort of contextual feature C obtains, then it is also true that one can report this by uttering 'I report that the enemy is in flight' only if C obtains. And unless he believes in a very powerful kind of word magic, no one will suppose that the mere use of the performative prefix 'I report that . . .' could guarantee the presence of C.

One reason why contextual features are theoretically indispensable is that conversations always have a beginning, and that what S says is, in most cases anyway, not self-authenticating, i.e. not such that the nature of what is said guarantees its own truth. The fact that what S says is that the enemy is in flight, for instance, does not guarantee that what is said is true. Of course, such a claim can be supported by another, and so on, but such claims have to terminate somewhere. One reasonable terminus would be with a claim which is very likely to be true given S's opportunities for observation, or given that what he says concerns matters which he can be expected to have personal knowledge of, etc. And the fact that we do often accept testimony in such circumstances as these throws some light on a question which is rarely discussed, but which ought to be very puzzling, namely, why it is that we rarely use explicit performatives.

Part of the answer is that speakers often employ the first of the two ways discussed of making force explicit in preference to the second. That is, they tell their audiences that certain things are the case which, if they are, means that they are in a position to perform various acts. Of course, a man's audience need not accept what it is told. But if he says that he has just come from a meeting at which he spoke personally, there is every reason to accept that he has, since he can be expected to know about his recent whereabouts and what he did. Further, if it is accepted that he was at the meeting, then it has to be accepted that he is in a position to inform us about, or report upon, what happened at the meeting, and utterances of his about events at the meeting, will readily be accepted as reports. There will be no need to make this explicit.

Thus, to accept certain claims made by S will be to accept that a context exists in which he can perform a range of illocutionary acts, since the truth of his claim guarantees the presence of various relevant features. This is important because it means that A's beliefs about what belongs to the context of S's utterance can be augmented by his acceptance of things which S has said to him. It follows that a context for the utterance of each sentence does not have to be given *de novo*, quite independently of the rest of a discourse. If it did, the notion of context could not possibly bear the weight a theory like mine puts on it. Fortunately, however, A's acceptance of what S has said to him can significantly determine his beliefs about the nature of the context, and hence his beliefs about the nature of future sayings. Thus, it is easy to see how once an initial piece of testimony has been accepted, the existence of an increasingly rich context can come to be recognized, and with it the possibility of recognizing the performance of an increasingly rich range of illocutionary acts.

WORKS CITED

ALSTON, W. P.   1964 *The Philosophy of Language*, Prentice Hall.

1968 'Meaning and Use', in *The Theory of Meaning*, ed. G. H. R. Parkinson, Oxford Univ. Press.

1971 'How does one tell whether a word has one, several or many senses', in *Semantics: An Interdisciplinary Reader*, ed. D. Steinberg and L. Jakobovits, Cambridge Univ. Press.

ANDERSON, S. R.   1971 'On the Linguistic Status of the Performative/Constative Distinction', *Indiana Linguistics Club*.

ÅQVIST L.   1965 *A New Approach to the Logical Theory of Interrogatives*, Uppsala Univ. Press.

ARMSTRONG, D.   1971 'Meaning and Communication', *Philosophical Review*, LXXX, 427.

ATTFIELD, R. AND DURRANT, M.   1973 'The Irreducibility of Meaning', *Nous*, VII. 282.

AUSTIN, J. L.   1961 *Philosophical Papers*, ed. J. O. Urmson and G. J. Warnock, *Clarendon Press*.

1962 *How To Do Things With Words*, ed. J. O. Urmson, Clarendon Press.

BAKER, C. L.   1970 'Notes on The Description of English Questions: The Role of an Abstract Question Morpheme', *Foundationsof Language*, VI. 197. Reprinted in *Semantic Syntax*, ed. P. Seuren, Oxford Univ. Press, 1974.

BELL, M.   1975 'Questioning', *Philosophical Quarterly*, XXV. 193.

BENNETT, J.   1973 'The Meaning-Nominalist Strategy', *Foundations of Language*, X. 141.

BOYD, J. AND THORNE, J. P.   1969 'The Semantics of Modal Verbs', *Journal of Linguistics*, V. 57.

BROMBERGER, SYLVAIN   1966 'Questions', *Journal of Philosophy*, LXIII. 597.

CASTANEDA, HECTOR-NERI   1963 'Imperatives, Decisions and Oughts', in *Morality and The Language of Conduct*, ed. Hector-Neri Castañeda and George Nakhnikian, Wayne State Univ. Press, p. 219.

CLARKE, D. S., JR.   1969 'Mood Constancy in Mixed Interences', *Analysis*, XXX. 100.

COHEN, J. L.   1964 'Do Illocutionary Forces Exist?', *Philosophical Quarterly*, XIV. 118.

COHEN, TED   1973 'Illocutions and Perlocutions', *Foundations of Language*, IX. 492.

COOPER, D. E.   1972 'Meaning and Illocutions', *American Philosophical Quarterly*, IX. 69.

DUMMETT, M.   1958 'Truth', *Proceedings of the Aristotelian Society*, LIX. 141.

  1973 *Frege: Philosophy of Language*, Duckworth.

DURRANT, M. AND ATTFIELD, R.   1973 'The Irreducibility of Meaning', *Nous*, VII. 282.

EDGLEY, R.   1969 *Reason in Theory and Practice*, Hutchinson's University Library.

FILLIMORE, C.   1972 'Subjects, Speakers, and Roles', in *Semantics of Natural Language*, ed. D. Davidson and G. Harman, Reidel, p. 1.

FINE, K.   1973 'Some Ross Type Paradoxes', mimeo.

FRASER, B.   1971 'An Examination of the Performative Analysis', *Indiana Linguistics Club*.

FURBERG, M.   1971 *Saying and Meaning: A main theme in J. L. Austin's Philosophy*, Blackwell.

GARDINER, A.   1951 *Speech and Language*, Clarendon Press.

GEACH, P. T.   1963 'Imperative Inference', *Analysis Supplement*, XXIII.37.

  1965 'Assertion', *Philosophical Review*, LXXIV. 449.

GRICE, H. P.   1957 'Meaning', *Philosophical Review*, LXVI. 377.

  1969 'Utterer's Meaning and Intentions', *Philosophical Review*, LXXVIII.147.

HARE, R. M.   1949 'Imperative Sentences', *Mind*, LVIII. 21. This, together with Hare (1967), was reprinted in Hare (1971). My references are to this collection.

  1952 *The Language of Morals*, Clarendon Press.

	1967	'Some Alleged Differences Between Imperatives and Indicatives', *Mind*, LXXVI.309.
	1970	'Meaning and Speech Acts', *Philosophical Review*, LXXIX.3.
	1971	*Practical Inferences*, MacMillan.
HOFSTADTER, A. AND McKINSEY, J. J. C.	1939	'On the Logic of Imperatives', *Philosophy of Science*, p. 446.
HOLDCROFT, D.	1968	'Meaning and Illocutionary Acts', in *The Theory of Meaning*, ed. G. H. R. Parkinson, Oxford Univ. Press, p. 166.
	1974	'Doubts About The Locutionary/Illocutionary Distinction', *International Studies in Philosophy*.
	1976	'Forms of Indirect Communication: an Outline', *Philosophy and Rhetoric*.
HOUSEHOLDER, F. W.	1971	*Linguistic Speculations*, Cambridge Univ. Press.
KAMP, H.	1973	'Free Choice Permission', *Proceedings of the Aristotelian Society*, LXXIV.57.
KATZ, J. J. AND POSTAL, P.	1964	*An Integrated Theory of Linguistic Descriptions*, M.I.T. Press.
KENNY, A. J.	1966	'Practical Inference', *Analysis*, XXVI.65.
KIERKEGAARD, S.	1966	*The Concept of Irony: With Constant Reference To Socrates*, trans. Lee M. Capel, Collins.
KIMBALL, J.	1973	*The Formal Theory of Grammar*, Prentice Hall.
LAKOFF, GEORGE	1972	'Linguistics and Natural Logic', in *Semantics of Natural Language*, ed. D. Davidson and G. Harman, Reidel, p. 545.
	1976	'Pragmatics in Natural Logic', in *Formal Semantics of Natural Language*, ed. E. L. Keenan, Cambridge Univ. Press, p. 253.
LAKOFF, ROBIN	1969	'Some Reasons Why There Can't be Any *some-any* Rule', *Language*, XLV.608.
LEMMON, E. J.	1962	'On Sentences Verifiable By Their Use', *Analysis*, XXII.86.
LEWIS, D.	1969	*Convention: a Philosophical Study*, Harvard Univ. Press.

1972 'General Semantics', in *Semantics of Natural Language*, ed. D. Davidson and G. Harman, Reidel, p. 169.

MACKIE, J. L.   1962 'Counterfactuals and Causal Laws', in *Analytical Philosophy*, ed. R. J. Butler, Blackwell, p. 66.

McCAWLEY, J. D.   1968 'The Role of Semantics in a Grammar', in *Universals in Linguistic Theory*, ed. E. Bach and R. Harms, Holt, Rinehart, and Winston, p. 124.

McKINSEY, J. J. C. AND HOFSTADTER, A.   1939 'On the Logic of Imperatives', *Philosophy of Science*, p. 446.

MUECKE, D. C.   1970 *Irony*, Methuen.

PALMER, F. R.   1965 *The English Verb*, Longmans.

PHILLIPS-GRIFFITHS, A. ed.   1967 *Knowledge and Belief*, Oxford Univ. Press.

POSTAL, P. AND KATZ, J. J.   1964 *An Integrated Theory of Linguistic Descriptions*, M.I.T. Press.

RICHARDS, BARRY   1971 'Searle on Meaning and Speech Acts', *Foundations of Language*, VII.519.

RICHARDS, D. A. J.   1971 *A Theory of Reasons For Action*, Clarendon Press.

ROSS, ALF   1944 'Imperatives and Logic', *Philosophy of Science*, p. 30.

   1968 *Directives and Norms*, Routledge and Kegan Paul.

ROSS, J. R.   1970 'On Declarative Sentences', in *Readings in English Transformational Grammar*, ed. R. Jacobs and P. Rosenbaum, Ginn and Co., p. 222.

SCHIFFER, S.   1972 *Meaning*, Clarendon Press.

SEARLE, J. R.   1968 'Austin on Locutionary and Illocutionary Acts', *Philosophical Review*, LXXVII. 405.

   1969 *Speech Acts*, Cambridge Univ. Press.

SELLARS, W.   1963 'Imperatives, Intentions and The Logic of "Ought"', in *Morality and The Language of Conduct*, ed. Hector-Neri Castañeda and George Nakhnikian, Wayne State Univ. Press, p. 159.

STENIUS, E.   1969 'Mood and Language Game', in *Philo-*

sophical Logic, ed. J. W. Davis, D. J. Hockney, and W. K. Wilson, Reidel, p. 251.

STRAWSON, P. F.　1964 'Intention and Convention in Speech Acts', *Philosophical Review*, LXXIII.439.

1969 'Meaning & Truth', Clarendon Press.

1970 'Phrase et acte de parole', *Langages*, 1970.

THORNE, J. P. AND BOYD, J.　1969 'The Semantics of Modal Verbs', *Journal of Linguistics*, V.57.

WARNOCK, G. J.　1971 'Hare on Meaning and Speech Acts', *Philosophical Review*, LXXX.

1973 'Some Types of Performative Utterance' in *Essays on J. L. Austin*, ed. I. Berlin *et al.*, Clarendon Press, p. 69.

WILLIAMS, B.　1963 'Imperative Inference', *Analysis Supplement*, XXIII.30.

VENDLER, ZENO　1967 *Adjectives and Nominalisations*, Mouton.

1968 *Linguistics in Philosophy*, Cornell Univ. Press.

1972 *Res Cogitans*, Cornell Univ. Press.

INDEX